BURGUNDY

AND ITS WINES

BURGUNDY

AND ITS WINES

NICHOLAS FAITH

PHOTOGRAPHY BY ANDY KATZ

DUNCAN BAIRD PUBLISHERS

LONDON

Burgundy and its Wines
An appreciation by Nicholas Faith
Photography by Andy Katz

First published in the United Kingdom
and Ireland in 2002 by
Duncan Baird Publishers Ltd
Sixth Floor, Castle House
75–76 Wells Street
London W1T 3QH

Conceived, created and designed by
Duncan Baird Publishers

Managing Editor: Christopher Westhorp
Editor: James Hodgson
Managing Designer: Manisha Patel
Designer: Emma Rose
Picture research: Julia Brown and Alice Gillespie
Commissioned maps: Neil Gower

British Library Cataloguing-in-Publication Data:
A catalogue record for this book is available from
the British Library

10 9 8 7 6 5 4 3 2 1

ISBN: 1-903296-78-1

Typeset in Apollo MT
Colour reproduction by Scanhouse, Malaysia
Printed in China by Imago

NOTES
The following abbreviations are used in this book:
BCE Before the Common Era (the equivalent of BC)
CE Common Era (the equivalent of AD)
TGV Train à Grande Vitesse (high-speed train)

Measurements are shown in metric units –
below are approximate imperial equivalents:
1 hectare = 2.5 acres
1 kilogram = 2.2 pounds
1 kilometre = 0.6 of a mile

CONTENTS

INTRODUCTION BY ROBERT M. PARKER, JR.

While Andy Katz's exquisite photographs of Burgundy easily stand on their own, it really isn't appropriate to look at them without a brief understanding of the unique qualities of this area. The Burgundy area of eastern France encompasses five basic regions: Chablis, Côte d'Or (which contains the two famous golden slopes called the Côte de Beaune and Côte de Nuits), Côte Chalonnaise, Mâconnais and Beaujolais. Unlike Bordeaux, which is bounded on one side by the ocean and on the other by the Gironde river, Burgundy has no major bodies of water to affect its climate and consequently is shaped significantly by the west winds that buffet it, along with the significant rainfall and devastating hailstorms they often carry. While this can be a detriment to the wine producers of the region, Burgundy's northerly latitude also provides for longer hours of daylight during the important summer growing months, so with dry, sunny weather from the beginning of September onward, a fine crop can still be produced.

The majority of the region's soil is made up of kimmeridge clay and limestone. In Chablis, this soil and its cousin, the portlandian limestone, are ideal for Chardonnay grapes. The famed Côte d'Or, which for many connoisseurs of Burgundy is that region's beginning and end, is essentially a limestone ridge representing the eastern edge of a calcareous plateau that empties into the Saône river basin. The northern half, the Côte de Nuits, has an easterly orientation that gradually shifts toward a more southeasterly exposure. This ridge runs for about 50 kilometres between Marsannay and Santenay. In the Côte Chalonnaise, the limestone ridge begins to break up into a chain of small hills that have limestone subsoils with clay/sand topsoils that are occasionally enriched with iron deposits. However, the underlying limestone strata are still present and continue not only through the Côte Chalonnaise, but also through the pastoral, rolling hills of the neighbouring Mâconnais region, giving way finally to the granite-based soils of the Beaujolais region.

Geologists believe the limestone shelf now called the Côte d'Or was formed more than 150 million years ago, well before man appeared on the scene. During what is called the Jurassic period (between 135 and 195 million years ago), the geological face of Burgundy began to take shape. Formed during this epoch were the petrified remains of sea life, compressed over time with a calcareous mudstone, as well as the rock that resulted from the precipitation of lime from the sea water that then covered Burgundy. The limestone rocks sprinkled with marlstone constitute the backbone of the various hillsides and most renowned vineyard sites of not only the Côte d'Or, but

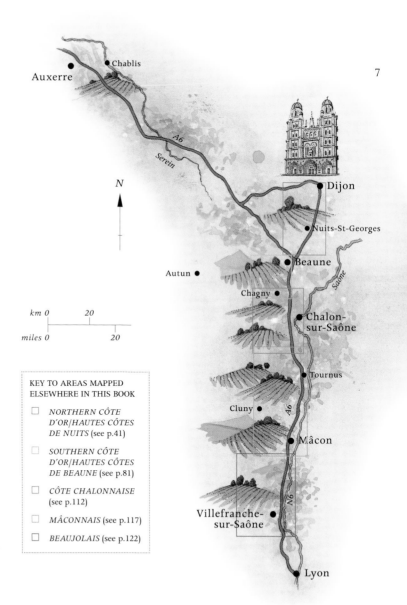

KEY TO AREAS MAPPED
ELSEWHERE IN THIS BOOK

☐ *NORTHERN CÔTE D'OR/HAUTES CÔTES DE NUITS* (see p.41)

☐ *SOUTHERN CÔTE D'OR/HAUTES CÔTES DE BEAUNE* (see p.81)

☐ *CÔTE CHALONNAISE* (see p.112)

☐ *MÂCONNAIS* (see p.117)

☐ *BEAUJOLAIS* (see p.122)

8 also the slopes of Chablis, the Côte Chalonnaise and the Mâconnais.

The climate and the soil are two of the distinct features of Burgundy; the people and their culture are another. Viticulture is believed to have been launched in Burgundy by either the Greeks or the Romans. There was a thriving Greek settlement at Marseilles around 600BCE, leading some observers to surmise that the Greeks travelling through the Rhône Valley were responsible for the vineyards planted along the hillsides of the Rhône river as well as those further north in Burgundy. Other observers claim that viticulture was brought to Burgundy by the Romans, whose influence can be seen in the architectural ruins that archaeologists have unearthed. With Caesar's conquest of Gaul in 52BCE came a degree of stability and civilization that provided the necessary economy to foster the production of wine, and it would be unlikely that

the wine-loving Romans would not have encouraged vineyard development and wine production in the territory. However, the absence of any hard evidence makes such theories conjectural.

Burgundy came into its own during the Middle Ages, with the flourishing of the Catholic Church, and more specifically under the Benedictine order of Cluny. In 1098 a Benedictine order, the Cistercians, was established at the abbey of Cîteaux in a desolate area just to the east of the village of Nuits-St-Georges. These monks were renowned for their religious enthusiasm, work ethic, spartan lifestyle and adherence to physically exhausting hard labour. This philosophy apparently led to the Cistercians' decision to cultivate the poor, infertile, rocky soil of what today is known as the Côte d'Or. This stretch of limestone hillsides had long proved unsuitable for crops, but the Cistercians, with their commitment to back-breaking labour, believed the vine could be cultivated and quality wine produced.

The expansion and empire building of the ecclesiastic orders in Burgundy was impressive, even by today's standards. In 1141 the nuns of the Cistercian abbey of Notre Dame du Tart purchased a vineyard in Morey-St-Denis that became known as the Clos de Tart. It remained under their control until the French Revolution. The Cistercians also launched a branch of their order at the Clos de Vougeot, which hundreds of years later became part of the elaborate *appellation* system imposed on all of the best winemaking regions of France. Ultimately the religious orders controlled much of the wine that was shipped to the government in Paris, principally because France's other renowned viticultural region, Bordeaux, was at that time controlled by the English and their desire for claret.

The height of Burgundy's power, historically referred to as the Golden Age, ranged from the middle of the 14th century to the middle of the 15th century. During this era the great dukes of Burgundy controlled not only Burgundy, but also the majority of northern France and large portions of what is now Belgium, the Netherlands and Luxembourg. This period witnessed an extraordinary flourishing of art, architecture and music. Under the dukes, the huge monastic orders prospered even further. They were the beneficiaries of large land grants and were encouraged by the dukes to build great abbeys and cathedrals. To no one's surprise, the Church's chief worldly export, wine, prospered well.

The French Revolution of 1789 fundamentally altered the landscape of Burgundy, tearing apart most of the gigantic wine estates owned by the wealthy and the monastic orders. Subsequently, the Napoleonic-Sallic Code increased the fragmentation of Burgundy's vineyards. This code required that upon the death of a parent the land be divided equally among all sons. With each new generation Burgundy's lands became more and more fragmented, each parcel owned by a different person.

10 Today's Burgundy is, therefore, distressingly difficult to grasp and comprehend. This multiple ownership of the same vineyard reaches its preposterous, dizzyingly frustrating absurdity with the great vineyard of Clos Vougeot, which possesses 50 hectares and 77-plus landowners. One hardly needs to be reminded of the infinite number of variations in quality that can occur from the same vineyard when the wine is made by as many as six dozen different producers.

In the late 19th century, Burgundy was ravaged by the phylloxera epidemic that devastated all of Europe's vineyards. While Burgundy did escape serious damage during World War I, the area was occupied by Germany during World War II. In late 1944 and early 1945, there were some small but fierce battles between the Allied forces and the retreating Germans, particularly in the Côte de Beaune. An endearing story of a French commander has emerged from the skirmishes of the last years of World War II. The commander apparently delayed his attack on the retreating Germans for fear of damaging the best Premier Cru and Grand Cru vineyards of Chassagne-Montrachet, Puligny-Montrachet and Meursault. When he was subsequently apprised the Germans were occupying the lower slopes, or those vineyards not entitled to Premier Cru or Grand Cru status, he immediately ordered his soldiers to attack the German positions.

This is the rich history that comes to mind when I view Andy Katz's photos, and I wonder about the timelessness of nature. While the vines and people may have changed over the centuries, the soil and the method of cultivating grapes to wine really hasn't. The walls that border the vineyard may be only five hundred years old, but the rocks they contain remember dinosaurs and other creatures of which we can only dream. And that little shady spot where the oak bows over the wall looks like the perfect place to sit, drink a glass of Beaujolais, and contemplate it all. Please enjoy these incomparable photos, which brought new meaning to me, of a region I know and love.

CHAPTER ONE

WHY BURGUNDY?

FOR TWO THOUSAND YEARS THE CÔTE D'OR IN BURGUNDY HAS BEEN FAMOUS FOR SOME OF THE FINEST WINES ON THE PLANET. THEY ARE THE MOST DISTINGUISHED PRODUCTS OF TWO MAJOR GRAPE VARIETIES: THE SUPPLE CHARDONNAY AND THE FICKLE PINOT NOIR. THEIR QUALITY CAN BE EXPLAINED PARTLY BY THE UNIQUE GEOGRAPHY AND GEOLOGY OF THE EAST-FACING SLOPES ON WHICH THEY ARE GROWN, AND PARTLY BY THE PATIENT EFFORTS OF DEVOTED WINEMAKERS THROUGH THE CENTURIES. THE FAME OF THE WINES SPREAD ALL OVER THE CIVILIZED WORLD BECAUSE THE DUCHY OF BURGUNDY — AS IT WAS KNOWN FOR HUNDREDS OF YEARS — WAS AT THE CENTRE OF WESTERN EUROPE'S TRADE ROUTES. DURING THE 14TH AND 15TH CENTURIES, BURGUNDY WAS AN INDEPENDENT STATE — AND FOR MUCH LONGER A CENTRE FOR MONASTIC ORDERS THAT OWNED THE VINES AND GUARANTEED NOT ONLY THE QUALITY OF THE WINE BUT ALSO A WIDE DIFFUSION THROUGHOUT CHRISTENDOM.

14 Until the mid-19th century Burgundy was the only one of the world's vineyards not conveniently placed on navigable waters whose wines were appreciated far outside its own region. For, until the railway age, the only economic method of transporting wines or spirits was by water. And Burgundy is miles away from the River Saône, which itself was not much use when carrying wines to the markets of Paris and the Low Countries. So the wines of Burgundy had to be something special: they had to justify the enormous expense (and considerable risk) of overland transport.

The list of Burgundy-lovers resounds throughout French history. For most of his long life, Louis XIV drank Burgundy. Napoleon – not really a connoisseur – drank Chambertin much diluted with water, while General de Gaulle was also fond of Burgundy – too much so for his wife, Tante Yvonne, who kept a beady eye on his consumption, though she allowed him a bottle after the loss of the referendum that led to his resignation in 1969.

"We musn't let them get me down," said the 79-year-old statesman, "fetch me a bottle of one of Méo's wines" – a 1964 Clos Vougeot.

Not surprisingly, there have been innumerable eulogies to the wines of the region down the centuries. One of the best came from Cyrus Redding, the ultra-critical Victorian wine merchant and writer: "Burgundy," he wrote, "is perhaps the most perfect of all the known wines in the qualities that are deemed most essential to vinous perfection. The flavour is delicious, the bouquet exquisite and the superior delicacy which it possesses justly entitles it to be held first in estimation of all the red wines grown … fine colour, enough of spirit raciness, good body, great fineness, an aroma of bouquet very powerful, strong in odour, and that peculiar taste which

A wine festival at Joigny in north-western Burgundy, as portrayed by an unknown artist in the early 19th century. Note the early wine bottles – and Bacchus in the cart attended by village maidens.

so remarkably distinguishes them from all the other wines of France." And I certainly would not argue with that encomium.

Yet Burgundy is a very small vineyard, constituting a mere quarter of one per cent of world acreage and only six per cent of all the vineyards in France entitled to Appellation d'Origine Contrôlée (see p.48). Moreover, the wines that account for the region's reputation – 32 Grands Crus on the Côte d'Or between Dijon and Chagny – make up a mere one per cent of Burgundy's production, and the Premiers Crus – only slightly less grand – little more than a tenth (see box, opposite). The 53 villages entitled to have their names on the bottle account for a further quarter, so the bulk of the production is entitled only to the name of Burgundy – which should be, but regrettably isn't, a noble name in itself. The order

The Virgin Mary, as portrayed on one of the region's innumerable Gothic churches – this one at St-Romain in the Hautes Côtes.

of precedence is even more entrenched – an appropriate word – than in Bordeaux. In Burgundy it is the *terroir* – the peculiarly French combination of soil, subsoil and climate – that dictates reputation, so it is virtually impossible for wines from "lesser" *appellations*, like Pernand-

---

GRANDS CRUS, PREMIERS CRUS, ET CETERA

All wine regions have their hierarchies, and Burgundy is no different. Grands Crus – Burgundy's finest wines – are identified on the label merely by the name of their *lieu-dit*, or vineyard, since everyone is assumed to know which village they come from. Several of the villages, like Gevrey-Chambertin and Vosne-Romanée, changed their names to include the name of their most famous vineyard. Next in rank, the Premiers Crus carry further information – the village and the vineyard. Then come "village wines" with communal *appellations*. Lowest in the hierarchy is the grandly named Bourgogne Grand Ordinaire, the much-despised BGO. Two-thirds of Burgundy's wines are generic.

Vergelesses, to achieve the reputation, and thus the prices, reached by their more illustrious neighbours.

In the beginning, geologically speaking, came the Jurassic slopes, the key to the region's capacity to produce great wines. Originally, the region was covered by a shallow sea. Then, 150 million years ago, the shells became fossils, and by the time the sea finally receded, a mere 30 million years ago, in the Tertiary era when the Alps and Pyrenees were being created, the landscape had formed – a series of rough, unproductive limestone slopes. Over the millennia, the locals have dug out innumerable stones from the vineyards. The process continues: a few years ago I saw a giant bulldozer excavating a metre or more under the north part of the Clos de Vougeot and uncovering giant boulders left untouched by the efforts of previous centuries. You can still see the stones in piles (which the locals call *murgers*) and in dry-stone walls, more or less lovingly maintained, their entrances surmounted by curving lintels, the appropriate

18 doorways to individual chapels in the great cathedral of wine that is Burgundy.

Essentially, Burgundy is not complicated. The simplest map shows the slash of vineyards across the slopes of the Côte d'Or. The vines occupy a thin ribbon of land, seldom more than a kilometre wide, and they are rarely, if ever, grown below the Route Nationale (RN) 74, which heads south from Dijon, and marks the boundary of the vineyard. Only below the RN do we find the rich fields typical of rural France – flatlands that have been invaded by vines only in times of extreme prosperity, most notably in the course of the 19th century. The "Nationale" is an ancient route trodden these past two thousand years, so popular that it is now paralleled by an *autoroute* and a railway line. To watch a TGV from a vineyard famous for a thousand years is to appreciate the rationale, and the eternity, of Burgundian culture – its position as a crucial focal point amid the trade routes that had such a civilizing role before the coming of the railways.

Geographically, the Côte d'Or can be defined merely as stony slopes between the valley of the Saône and the Burgundian escarpment. These slopes are part of a chain that extends from the Elbe in northern Germany down to the Dordogne and Languedoc. But there is an important divide in the Côte d'Or: to the north of Dijon, the slopes are low and gentle; south of the city they are steeper, and, crucially, face due east to catch the morning sun.

As so often with fine vineyards, the soil is too poor to allow other crops to flourish, apart from junipers, stunted oak trees and the delicious wild garlic that sprouts between the vines (and why has no enterprising Burgundian chef used it to greater purpose?). Above the vine-line are the forests, crucial for protecting the vines from the winds (and now torn down, fatally changing the

A typical portal to a classy vineyard. This one is in Meursault – the vineyard is owned by the family of Jacques Prieur, while the wine is now (very well) made by Antonin Rodet.

microclimate). The weather is truly continental, with some of the harshest winters and stormiest summers in France. Nevertheless, in one of the most northerly major vineyards in the world, the grapes enjoy immensely long summer days, many of them sunny. For obvious reasons – they are above the clay of the valleys, yet not too high to be exposed to the winds that chill the summits – the finest vineyards are halfway up the hill, the meat in the middle of the sandwich.

To geography add two grape varieties: the now-universal Chardonnay and that finest, most unforgiving of black grapes, the Pinot Noir. Weirdly, there are many spots in Burgundy that seem to suit both varieties equally well. Historically, the Chardonnay was planted even in such unlikely places as Chambertin and the Clos de Vougeot (there is still one patch of Chardonnay just outside the

Winter bleakness on a road typical of France in general – and of Burgundy in particular.

sacred enclosure). Even today the proportion of white and red on the slopes behind Beaune is still changing.

It is typical of Burgundy, that most idiosyncratic of vineyards, that it should be dominated by the Pinot Noir, a variety that is itself quirky, difficult – the very image of capriciousness. It is not productive. It is subject to all sorts of diseases, it sulks, and in Burgundy, more often than not, it simply won't ripen. But when it does, the long summer days ensure that the grapes will have ripened properly, not through the injection of sudden bursts of heat as in warmer climates, but through a gentle process of ripening on the vine.

The preponderance of Pinot Noir is not new: as early as 1395 the then Duke of Burgundy promulgated a decree that sought to rid the province of the pesky Gamay in favour of the Pinot. Given the quality of the wines (and,

Woods like these provide crucial protection for the vines from cold, wet winds whistling down from the heights above the Côte d'Or.

to be crude, their prices) it is hardly surprising that the search after a Pinot Noir to match the Burgundians' has become something of a Quest for the Holy Grail for winemakers the world over.

The problem for non-Burgundians is that the Grail takes many different forms. It can be pale, almost lilac-blossom colour, ranging to much heartier, sweaty-saddle overtones. The aromas and the flavours of wines from adjacent communes (like Volnay and Pommard) vary from relatively firm, almost tough and tannic, to the smoothest, most aromatic, most velvety of wines. For me the ideal is a wine reminiscent of *griottes* (slightly unripe cherries), with a miraculous balance of fruit and acidity found nowhere else on the planet.

The picture was muddied by the portrayal of Burgundy as a relatively robust wine, an idea that owed everything to the addition of dollops of wine from the Rhône – hence the answer to the question, "What are the biggest cellars in Burgundy?", to which the reply was,

"the marshalling yards at Beaune". Here, wines from the Rhône – or even Algeria – were stored, then simply bottled and sent on their way as the produce of Burgundy. After 1973 the Common Market rules ensured that such wines could not be sold – above all abroad – as Burgundy. Today, the aim of too many Burgundian wine-makers seems to be to produce straightforwardly fruity, easy-drinking wines – which are not too difficult to imitate elsewhere in the world.

The same applies in spades to run-of-the-mill white wines produced from the ever-willing Chardonnay, whose wines are (almost) always drinkable, so that to many people the name Chardonnay is a byword for a harmless dry white wine. Today there is much less Chardonnay in Burgundy than in Australia, and under a third of the acreage to be found in California. The name came into general use only in the 19th century but the grape had already reigned supreme in Burgundy for centuries, under its old names of Norien Blanc and Pinot

24 Blanc – the latter emphasizing the family connection between it and the Pinot Noir (it is the offspring of two grapes native to north-eastern France, the Pinot Noir and the Gouais Blanc). They may all derive from the same grape, but the greatest white Burgundies come in two styles (three if you include the steely fruitiness of Chablis): the rich, full wines from Corton and the delicately aromatic wines made in Meursault and the two Montrachets south of Beaune. Nevertheless, they all need fermentation in wood to extract all the aromas.

Living uneasily in the shadow of these two "noble" varieties are two others: the white Aligoté found scattered throughout much of Burgundy; and the Gamay, grown in Beaujolais – and virtually nowhere else in the world. Both are fascinating, and have suffered badly from the reputation of their "nobler" brethren. Other, even more marginal, varieties on the wane – in Burgundy anyway – include the Melon de Bourgogne, which produces Muscadet, the Sacy once used by the Champenois as a base wine, and the César, whose name the relentless Burgundian propaganda machine attributed to Roman occupation. Some lost varieties, most obviously the Pinot Droit, could produce distinctive wines. Less regretted – except by a handful of growers in marginal communes – are the hybrids, like the infamous Noah – widely planted when quality was forgotten in the search for quantity after wartime shortages.

To geology, geography and vines add two thousand years of history. The first recorded description of the region's wines comes from Eumenius, a distinguished Roman citizen living at Autun. Unfortunately, he was trying to impress the taxman and so described the vineyard as being in a miserable state, the fame of its

RIGHT: *Note the narrowness of the rows between the vines, which stresses the grapes and thus helps concentrate the taste of their juice.* FAR RIGHT: *Harvest in Burgundy can be late, just as the leaves are starting to change colour.*

wines not justified by the age and exhaustion of the vines. The Romans bequeathed to the region not only vineyards, but also the feeling that it was an integral part of the backbone of western European civilization, which naturally included wine.

But the biggest boost to the wines of the region came in the early Middle Ages. Its source was clerical – not so much the secular clergy, but the great monastic foundations, above all that at Cluny, one of the most powerful religious centres in the whole of western Christendom between the 11th and 13th centuries, a primacy emphasized during the reign (not too strong a word) of Abbot Hugh at the end of the 11th century. But of course Cluny was not the only foundation: names like St Denis and St Vivant, incorporated in those of the communes

---

Tournus is home to the abbey of St Philibert, a stark Romanesque edifice dating back to the 10th century. The town, like many others in Burgundy, was a major monastic centre.

Morey and Romanée respectively, bear witness to congregations of monks who owned vineyards and appreciated their products.

Cluny is now a byword for the flowering of church architecture that culminated in the great Gothic cathedrals. It may seem blasphemous to compare the roles of Cluny in the fields of religion and wine, but the Europe-wide renown of the Cluniacs did provide the Burgundians with an unparalleled opportunity to advance the fame of their wines at a time when the only other major trade in wine was being conducted by the Bordelais, who were shipping vast quantities to Britain. But, a crucial difference: whereas the "clairets" drunk by the British were poor, thin, anonymous beverages, which turned into vinegar within a few months, the Burgundians found themselves in possession of a myriad of blessed plots, celebrated not for the quantity of the wines they produced but for their unique quality. Then, as now, their fame rested on an uncanny mix of elegance, fruit and a balance

28 between acidity and alkalinity, a perfection which no one else in the world has ever managed to achieve with the Pinot, or any other variety for that matter, and which even the Burgundians find difficult enough. Of course, being on a main trade route helped, and indeed if Burgundy had not been so situated its wines could never have become famous.

After they were banished and their lands seized during the French Revolution, the monks left another, intangible yet powerful, legacy – an incomparable publicity machine furnished not only by the prestigious "abbatial tables", where visiting dignitaries were served the region's finest wines, but also the numerous "daughter houses", monasteries scattered throughout Christendom, which provided a network to spread Burgundy's fame. By then the French aristocracy had joined the list of proprietors, as had numerous merchants, above all from Beaune, and they set the tone – sometimes to the detriment of the wines' quality – for a century and a half.

Their grip was slightly loosened by the vine-pest phylloxera, which led to the sale of so much of the vineyard to the ancestors of today's growers. After the Second World War, an increasing number, encouraged by foreign buyers – mostly American at first – began to sell their wines themselves rather than shipping them to merchants for blending. Phylloxera also led to a series of continuing revolutions in vineyard practice. Previously, vines had been planted closely – *en foule* (as a mass). The new grafted vines planted to replace those that had been killed were positioned in rows, so that horses could be used, whereas before everything had to be done by hand. Planting new vines broke a chain that in some cases could have lasted for a thousand years through *provignage* (replanting by bending over the stem of an existing vine into the ground). At the same time the absence of older vines encouraged a considerable reduction in the age at which it was thought best to drink the wines.

In the century since replanting, the story has been

even further complicated. To the infinite variations of the *terroirs* of Burgundy was added the Napoleonic inheritance laws, which ensured that every son of a family was entitled to a share of its assets. As a result the average vineyard covers little more than a hectare. The whole of the Côte d'Or resembles a palace housing hundreds of labyrinths – a never-ending complexity within apparent simplicity, a God-knows-how-many-dimensional map composed not only of the minute, yet crucial, variations in soil, subsoil and outlook from one patch – almost down to one row – of vines to the next, but also of the countless fissures imposed on this jigsaw by generations of family sub-divisions. It was Cyrus Redding who pinpointed the overwhelming importance of *terroir*, with its attendant geological and climatic peculiarities, as one of the two or three fundamental points that have marked out the wines

of Burgundy from all others. "The most delicious wine is sometimes grown on one little spot only," he wrote, "in the midst of vineyards which produce no others but of the ordinary quality: while in another place the product of a vineyard, in proportion to its surface, shall be incredibly small, yet of exquisite quality; at the same time, in the soil, aspect, treatment as to culture, and species of plant, there shall be no perceptible difference in the eye of the most experienced wine grower."

Inevitably, the Burgundian vineyard is different. As elsewhere in France the *lieu-dit* is a vineyard identified by a traditional name. Peculiarly Burgundian is the *climat*, well explained by Simon Loftus as "a vineyard

The first sign of autumn, before the leaves take on deeper shades of red and brown.

defined by topographical features which give an individual character to its wine: a *climat* may incorporate several *lieux-dits*" – the Premiers Crus in Puligny-Montrachet occupy 24 *lieux-dits*, which form 14 *climats*. The names, the distinctions, reflect man's struggle over hundreds of years to differentiate between, and thus define, two tiny patches of vines, separated by a narrow track, a ditch, a wall.

The fragmentation is reflected in local definitions, like an *ouvrée* – a mere twentieth of a hectare. There are also hundreds of the *journées*, found throughout rural France, each amounting to around a third of a hectare – the area a man could plough in a day (*jour*) before the arrival of tractors. To complicate matters further, families tend not to be content with cultivating their original plots but itch to have a few rows of vines in every

---

Leaving grass and plants between the rows of vines helps retain moisture in the soil during dry summers.

possible *appellation*, so an individual's holding may be split between a serious hectare or so and an *ouvrée* miles away. In many cases the owners – or the merchants, who are increasingly making wines from vines they do not own – take advantage of two arrangements: *métayage*, or share-cropping, by which the tiller of the soil takes half – or sometimes even less – of the product of his labours; and *fermage*, by which the vineyard is leased.

Over the past decade the average quality of the wines has improved thanks to the arrival of a new, better-educated generation of growers, and the increased importance of the oenologist, previously a secondary figure in Burgundy. A further boost to quality was provided by the fleeting presence of a Lebanese oenologist, Guy Accad. He was a leader in the trend toward cleaner grape-growing, which has resulted in a number of estates switching to bio-dynamic viticulture. Accad removed the chemical make-up that had hidden the real face of Pinot Noir. He claimed that he was a reactionary, starting his

32 work with a minute examination before bringing back into the vineyard the best practices of the past, by reducing the level of potassium in the soil – to release the grapes' acidity – and aiming to extract as much fruit and tannin as possible. These measures all encourage the grower to focus on the soil, in order to produce ripe, healthy grapes – the only base for fine wine. This first principle was rather neglected in the post-War concentration on the techniques of winemaking.

But even today, as one anonymous observer put it, "For every example where you cry 'Yippee, it tastes like it should!' you'll find far more wines which leave you staring blankly into the middle distance fingering your grievously abused wallet." Burgundy could still do better with its incomparable inheritance.

Winter in Volnay. In this classic layout, the slopes lead down to lesser vines grown on the flat lands on the other side of the route des vins, *which runs across the middle of the photograph.*

INTERLUDE:
A DUCHY AND ITS CAPITAL

34

Dijon was never itself a city of wine, but nevertheless played an essential role as a symbol of the greatness of the region and thus of its wines. For Dijon was the capital of the Duchy of Burgundy – for hundreds of years until 1477 a proudly independent state, its wealth and creativity visible through the city, above all in the Palais des Ducs, surrounded by streets demonstrating the style and dignity of the duchy in its heyday. Burgundy lay at the heart of the "Middle Kingdom", the buffer between the two most powerful dynasties in western Europe: to the west the ever-ambitious kings of France; to the east the Holy Roman Emperors. In the 15th century, the golden age of the independent duchy, the dukes' writ ran northward from the Swiss frontier to include much of what is now Holland and Belgium.

Burgundy's wines relied on the patronage of its dukes, for before the 19th century the reputation of

wines was made by the world's rulers. Three of these favoured wines are still famous: "Imperial Tokay", the preferred drink of the Hapsburg emperors in Vienna; the wine from the Vega Sicilia estate, drunk at the court of Spain; and the Burgundies endorsed by the dukes in Dijon. Because the quantity and variety of these latter wines were greater than the other two, and, moreover, because Burgundy was a focal point on the trade routes of northern Europe, their fame spread more widely. This advantage was consolidated with the coming of the railways, which provided a convenient means of transport for wines from land-locked regions like Burgundy. The Burgundians were lucky: not only did the monks give their blessing to the wines but the dukes of Burgundy

---

Joyous gargoyles on the church of Notre-Dame, a masterpiece of Gothic architecture in Dijon.

initiated a long-lasting tradition – the use of dinners, where the wine flowed, as occasions for pomp and circumstance. The custom is maintained to this day, except that the dinners now demonstrate not the power of the dukes, but the qualities of the wines produced in their former dominion.

Yet Burgundy was, essentially, French from the earliest times. It was at Bibracte, in the heart of the region, that Vercingetorix rallied the tribes of ancient Gaul against the Romans. He was unsuccessful. But no matter. He was the first demonstration of French national consciousness – an example to his successors, from Asterix to General de Gaulle. This meant that the French could never treat the wines of the province as being "foreign".

So, from the beginning, and thanks to the existence and the splendour of the duchy and its rulers, Burgundy's wines were both French and yet, historically, had enormous appeal in the duchy's former possessions, which remain faithful customers even today.

The magnificence of 15th-century Burgundy: this illuminated manuscript shows Charles the Bold, the last Duke of Burgundy, presiding over a conclave of the Order of the Golden Fleece. The ill-fated Charles was to die in battle at Nancy in 1477.

CHAPTER TWO

THE ROYAL ROAD TO ROMANÉE-CONTI

THE SLOPES BETWEEN DIJON AND BEAUNE PRODUCE MOST OF THE TRULY GREAT RED WINES OF BURGUNDY.

BY FAR THE FINEST ARE THE WINES OF UNIQUE ELEGANCE FROM THE DOMAINE DE LA ROMANÉE-CONTI,

NAMED AFTER AN 18TH-CENTURY PRINCE. THE ALMOST EQUALLY FAMOUS CLOS DE VOUGEOT IS A DIFFER-

ENT PROPOSITION, BECAUSE, AS A CONSEQUENCE OF FRENCH INHERITANCE LAWS, ITS 50 HECTARES ARE

DIVIDED BETWEEN 80 OR SO OWNERS, RESULTING IN WINES OF UNEVEN QUALITY. THE FORMER ABBEY THERE

HOUSES THE CHEVALIERS DU TASTEVIN, WHOSE SPLENDID BANQUETS DEMONSTRATE TO THE FULL THE

CAPACITY OF THE BURGUNDIANS TO ENJOY THEMSELVES — AND TO ENTERTAIN ROYALLY. BUT PERHAPS

THE SINGLE MOST REMARKABLE EXAMPLE OF BURGUNDY'S HERITAGE IS THE HILL OF CORTON, ONCE OWNED

BY THE EMPEROR CHARLEMAGNE, FOUNDER OF THE IDEA OF EUROPEAN UNION BACK IN THE EIGHTH

CENTURY. CORTON IS STILL PRODUCING WHITE WINES OF AN ADMIRABLE POWER AND RICHNESS.

The Côte d'Or stretches south from Dijon in a series of villages, all huddled together so as not to impinge on the precious vineyards, their inhabitants quirky when not impossible. The villages are divided by combes (short valleys cut into the ridge), their rocky slopes a reminder of the tough subsoil that lies beneath the whole Côte. Rightly, Jean-François Bazin (see p.144) calls the *route des vins* – parallel to the main N74 but a kilometre or more above it – "Burgundy's Champs Élysées". There is simply nowhere else on Earth where so slim a strip of vineyards contains so many names that are not just famous, but sacred to anyone with the remotest interest in wine.

Traditionally, the Côte has been divided between the Côte de Nuits, which runs south from Dijon as far as the quarries at Comblanchien (whose marble was used for the Paris Opéra and Orly airport), and the Côte de Beaune,

---

In full flower, this stag's-horn sumach provides an arresting counterpoint to the grey wall behind it.

which continues south, via Beaune, to Chagny. This division does not imply a distinction between the wines – the wines of Gevrey-Chambertin, say, have more in common with those of Pommard, south of Beaune, than they do with those of Gevrey's neighbour Vosne-Romanée. However, there is a social difference: to the south the vineyards were owned, or at least dominated, by the merchants of Beaune; to the north it was the growers who prevailed, because the inhabitants of Dijon, the nearest large town, were not much involved in the wine business.

Bazin talks about his native village of Gevrey-Chambertin (there are two villages: one on the main road, the other on the *route des vins*) as forming the overture to the "grande route", ignoring the wines of Marsannay and Chenôve closer to Dijon. To me, in a poetic mood for once, the commune's wines resemble rather a Beethoven symphony – strong, complex, infinitely varied. For, as all along the Côte d'Or's concave slopes, shaped as they are like a long parabola concentrating the summer sun,

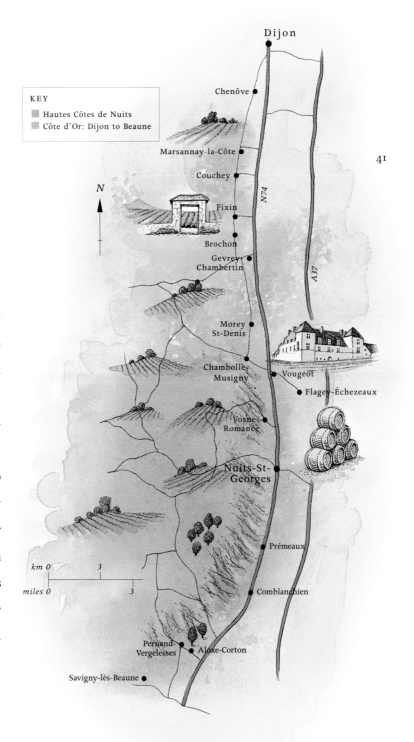

KEY

Hautes Côtes de Nuits
Côte d'Or: Dijon to Beaune

Dijon

Chenôve

Marsannay-la-Côte

Couchey

N74

A37

Fixin

Brochon

Gevrey-Chambertin

Morey-St-Denis

Chambolle-Musigny

Vougeot

Flagey-Échezeaux

Vosne-Romanée

Nuits-St-Georges

Prémeaux

Comblanchien

Pernand-Vergelesses

Aloxe-Corton

Savigny-lès-Beaune

N

km 0   3

miles 0   3

geology can provide only a partial explanation for the infinite variations of the wines within a single commune. In the words of André Védel: "Pedology [the science of soils] cannot explain the differences between the wines of Chambolle and those of Gevrey, and we know nothing of the nuances which distinguish the wines from Chambertin from those produced in Latricières or Mazis," – all three within Chambertin – "whose soil structure appears the same."

But then Gevrey-Chambertin has always been special. The château of Gevrey was the "fortified cellar" of the abbots of Cluny who stored their wines there. The distinctions between the many wines of the commune appeared early on. The name of Gevrey appears for the first time around 640CE, in a document recording the

FAR LEFT: *A contrast typical of Burgundy – a mirror to guide motorists set by the side of a traditional gate.* LEFT: *Decoration Burgundy-style: neatly attractive but not – ever – ostentatious.*

gift of a vast estate by Almagaire, Duke of Burgundy, to the abbey of Bèze, founded ten years earlier. The gift encompassed vines and vineyards in the area of Gevrey, including the Clos de Bèze – the first mention of a specific vineyard in Burgundian history. For me, the Clos de Bèze distils the whole history of Burgundy, and I find it infinitely moving to stroll through its vines, aware that its wines have been an inspiration for nearly fifteen hundred years. The continuity is not confined to Chambertin. In nearby Morey-St-Denis, the Clos de Tart, one of the rare vineyards to be controlled by a single owner, has changed hands only three times since the Middle Ages – and still boasts a 16th-century press.

The wines from Bèze were already much appreciated in the 11th century when the monks of Langres tried to buy the Clos. With the help of the pope, the abbey retained the precious plot for a further couple of centuries before poverty forced its sale in 1219. Even today, hundreds of years after the Clos de Bèze ceased to

44 have any connection with the abbey, the name remains, sanctified in the world of wine, if not of religion. And the earth is cultivated, the vines tended, by the very same families of growers, often working, as they always did, as share-croppers.

In the 15th and 16th centuries, more secular estates were built up. For example, Jean Moisson, a pious Dijon wine merchant, returned to his native village of Chambolle and built its first church in around 1450. In 1528 his granddaughter married Michel Millière, and brought with her the family vineyards in the village. The holding passed through seven generations until it was again transferred by marriage into the hands of François Melchior de Vogüé. Today the Domaine Comte Georges de Vogüé in Chambolle-Musigny is still run

A pictorial summary of the Burgundian landscape at Morey-St-Denis: dry-stone walls, gentle slopes and a collection of houses crowded together so as not to take too much land from the vines.

46 by one of Moisson's descendants, Élisabeth, Baronne Bertrand de la Doucette.

By the early 17th century, the monks were leasing their precious vines to families of *parlementaires*, France's usually wealthy legal aristocracy. The *parlementaires* of Dijon were a distinguished group, among them Bossuet (the learned bishop who first described England as "perfidious Albion"), Rameau, Buffon and the Président des Brosses. The whole of the Côte d'Or, right down to the most obscure villages, is studded with the handsome residences they built. For buying a vineyard in Burgundy was frightfully fashionable. But over the past hundred and fifty years more typical have been families like the Marions. France's inheritance laws have split their vineyards, while judicious marriages have added other holdings.

Many of these characters have sought – and found – fame and fortune outside Burgundy before returning to provide capital and worldly expertise to the region. For example, within Burgundy Frédéric Lescure is known as the owner of the Clos des Chapitres but is famous worldwide as the inventor of the pressure cooker. Jacques Seysses was born with a silver spoon in his mouth. His father ran Belin biscuits, and he himself was naturally friendly with most of Paris's major restaurateurs. After a playboy youth Seysses married (an American girl) and settled down on a domaine he has been running now for more than a quarter of a century. Or consider the Méo family. Jean Méo, a distinguished supporter of General de Gaulle, inherited the estate of Étienne Camuzet, who had served the Côte d'Or as its deputy from 1902 to 1932. It must have seemed most unlikely that his son Jean-Nicolas, a graduate of France's leading business school, would return to his native village of Vosne-Romanée. Yet he, too, felt the attraction of the world of

Burgundians at home: this elegant façade is typical of the houses of the most illustrious growers on the Côte d'Or.

48 wine. After studying oenology at Dijon University, for the past decade he has devoted himself to running the family estate.

For less distinguished families of growers, the road to independence from the influence of the wine merchants could be a long one. At first they had their grapes vinified at the growing number of cooperatives. The one in Gevrey was founded in 1912. Like many of its counterparts, it flourished between the wars when it had 130 members and vinified over half the grapes from the commune. But now, equally typically, it has only a handful of members, with tiny holdings. Merely accumulating the small amount of capital required to buy a few rows of vines was often difficult. As an old lady of Gevrey told Jean-François Bazin: "In the 1950s we understood that we had to copy the Poles

and grow onions. So we did, producing two tons a year, and it was hard work, but it did allow us to buy four *ouvrées* of vines." A certain Georges Lignier had grander ambitions than his father, a loyal estate-worker: "Every time there was a sale I'd buy a bit of vineyard – I had a hell of a lot of nerve." Against the tradition of his class, he was even prepared to borrow. Sometimes the families succeeded beyond their wildest dreams. In the 1930s the Dugats hoped to vinify a mere three *pièces* (1,000 kg) of grapes each year. They now own a substantial estate.

Between the two world wars, the French state armed the peasantry with an essential tool by steadily introducing the Appellation d'Origine Contrôlée (AOC), which gave the producers the exclusive right to use the name of their wines, thus, in theory anyway, preventing fraudsters from abusing such sacred names as "Chablis" and "Beaune". Some of the more ambitious peasants were Poles, often immigrants who originally came to work in the mines at Monceau, over the hill from the Côte d'Or, before the Second World War. Stanislas Serafin arrived at the end of the 1930s and married a fellow Pole. After five years as a prisoner of war, he laboured for growers and now has a typical, four-hectare Burgundian

estate, worked by his son. Three-quarters of the estate is concentrated in Gevrey village, the remainder consisting of tiny holdings in some of the grander *appellations*. Jean Heresztyn arrived in 1932 to work, not in the mines, but in a sugar refinery. Through sheer hard work he now owns not only a domaine, but some of the most beautiful cellars on the Côte de Nuits.

In recent decades more and more estates have started to sell their wines directly. A classic illustration of this trend is provided by the Gros family estate (now divided in two) in Vosne-Romanée. For the formidable but friendly Mme Janine Gros – a former mayor of the village – the shift to direct selling is no accident. "It's all part of the fashion for authenticity, and, of course, the advent of American buyers and the opening of the motorway to Paris were also big factors. Forty years ago not all the growers were equipped technically to take advantage of their opportunities: they were making what were often bad wines from good grapes. Even I lacked confidence, I didn't think that I would be able to find customers for my best wines. The merchants could sell their blends cheaply, and then concentrate on their own holdings in

the best *crus* ... in our case the Richebourg was our spearhead. But the family name also counts – one must have one's own labels, and one must maintain standards, which is why we had to downgrade all of our 1975 vintage."

The only wine she finds difficult to sell is from the family's holding in the Clos de Vougeot: "The quality of the *terroir* varies so much, and there's simply too much of the wine." She's right, for the Clos, which at first sight seems a homogenous stretch of vines, is in fact one of the most extraordinary demonstrations of the idiosyncracies of the Côte d'Or. Broadly it is divided into three: the gravelly upper third around the château, the central fillet, and the bottom part nearest the road. This section is usually derided, somewhat unjustly – the soil is full of pebbles and thus just as suitable for vines as the slopes above. Unfortunately, recent road builders have ruined the

Drama Burgundy-style: a stormy sky over Clos Vougeot.

drainage with "improvements", which actually ended up blocking the drains. But the very varying quality of the wine is mainly due to the sheer number of proprietors.

The name Clos de Vougeot was finally established in the late 14th century – making it relatively recent by Burgundian standards. Until the Revolution it was home to a Benedictine abbey, the order purified by St Bernard of Clairvaux in the early 12th century. For hundreds of years the estate acted as a sort of vini-cultural laboratory-cum-school (among other methods they heated the fermenting must and added sugar well before Monsieur Chaptal introduced the practice more generally at the beginning of the 19th century). But the later monks were not fanatical about wine. Although the vineyards of all the region's abbeys came to more than 1,300 hectares when they were confiscated during the

Chorey-lès-Beaune: the deep-red charm of a typical small Burgundian château.

Revolution, the monks had diversified so widely that this constituted a tiny fraction of their estates. For example, the vines of the abbey of Cîteaux represented only a hundredth of the 10,000 hectares of agricultural land they owned in 1789.

Following the many revolutionary upheavals, the whole of the Clos de Vougeot fell into the hands of the Ouvrard family (see p.67). By 1889 it was owned by six merchant firms from Beaune. Thanks to endless subdivisions, the number of individual plots has risen from 15 or so in the late 19th century to more than 80 today. Inevitably, the wine lacks a distinct image, except that it is nearer to Chambertin in its inherent robustness than to the more elegant – and more adjacent – Chambolle or Vosne.

Today, the Clos de Vougeot is also closely associated with the splendid celebrations held there by the Confrérie des Chevaliers du Tastevin, the most effective propaganda machine anywhere in the world of wine. It,

like the system of AOCs, was a response to the economic crisis of the 1930s, which naturally hit the fine-wine business particularly hard. The "order" was founded by Georges Faiveley, of the Faiveley firm of wine merchants, and Camille Rodier, an author and member of another merchant family. Improbably, one of its inspirations was Charles Dickens' fictional Pickwick Club. It brought together many ideas for promoting the wines of Burgundy, including the "Trois Glorieuses" – the collective name for the Hospices de Beaune wine auction (see pp.72–7), the Paulée de Meursault (see p.85) and a dinner in the Château du Clos de Vougeot, all of which take place each year on the third weekend in November.

The idea of a *confrérie*, or fraternity, was simplicity itself: a group of locals providing splendid banquets at which lucky outsiders – either celebrities from all over the world or, more pragmatically, "missionaries" able to sell or promote the wines of Burgundy – were "inaugurated" as members of the order. A further stroke

54 of genius was to establish a branch in the United States as early as 1939. This emphasized the region's dependence over the years on the American market, especially after pioneers like Frank Shoonmaker, Colonel William Wildman and – after World War Two – Alexis Lichine started their regular visits to obtain wine. Lichine, in particular, prodded individual estates to bottle their own wines, because he refused to buy from merchants. Since its beginnings, the Confrérie has become an extraordinarily professional operation with a dozen or more banquets a year, and its example has been followed throughout France. Nevertheless, the genuine warmth of any occasion in Burgundy ensures that it outshines even the more glamorous equivalent in Bordeaux.

But the Mecca on the road from Dijon to Beaune is the Domaine de la Romanée-Conti (DRC). Unusually for Burgundy, Romanée-Conti came to fame only in 1760, when the estate was bought by the truly princely Prince de Conti who then publicized it throughout fashionable Paris. (A long-lasting, if totally unfounded, myth has it that he outbid Madame de Pompadour, the famous mistress of King Louis XV.) There is nothing to distinguish the vineyard – today perhaps the most famous (and most valuable) piece of agricultural real estate in the world – except a modest wall to

Sing along with the Chevaliers du Tastevin. And the sign? A French pun: Jamais en vain, toujours en vin – *"Never in vain, always in wine".*

prevent erosion, similar to a thousand others, and an equally modest stone carved with the sacred name. This tiny plot, a mere 1.8 hectares in size, is at the heart of Burgundy, surrounded by a group of scarcely less distinguished names, most also owned by the DRC. For two families, de Villaine and Leroy (the current proprietors of the estate), own all six hectares of La Tâche, as well as much of Romanée-St-Vivant, Grands Échezaux and Échezaux – and even two-thirds of a hectare of Le Montrachet.

The estate is superbly run by Aubert de Villaine, most modest of guardians of the vinous temple. He insists on strict discipline – the domaine was an early user of conveyor belts to sort out rotten grapes and it dries the staves for its casks in the open air for three full years. The result is wines of extraordinary depth and "vinosity", with a unique combination of elegance, richness and length.

A few miles south is the small town, and major wine centre, of Nuits-St-Georges, best known for its wine merchants. In the past many of them – with honourable exceptions like Faiveley and Labouré-Roi – were responsible for some of the most soupy, untypical wines to carry the sacred name of Burgundy. But the reason why the commune does not contain the Grand Crus which many observers consider its due has nothing to do with commercial bad habits: it is rather that, when the decisions were being made, a local dignitary deemed that the formation of an élite community at Nuits would be contrary to the democratic spirit of the vineyards of Burgundy.

Between Nuits and Beaune there is one last surprise – the splendid hill of Corton, its rounded south-facing slopes forming the single biggest Grand Cru in Burgundy, with 160 hectares of vines. Its chalky slopes, rich with iron, produce Burgundy's fleshiest, most characterful white wines, as well as a Grand Cru red. The name "Corton-Charlemagne" is not some piece of Burgundian bull, but has a real historical basis, for it was the first Holy Roman Emperor who provided the impetus for today's vineyards

56 back at the end of the eighth century. Charlemagne's grand-father, Charles Martel ("Hammer" of the Muslim invaders), had suspected the Church of collaborating with the infidels, so he confiscated some of their lands in Burgundy. But the grandson restored many of them, including, crucially for us, the estate of Aloxe-Corton.

This provided the first opportunity for the amazing Burgundian publicity machine, which ever since has exploited the *folklorique* with an unscrupulousness that no mere advertising agency would ever dare emulate. Just listen to the story of how the slopes of the hill of Corton, unlike any others for miles around, came to have their white vines. "Once upon a time, the slopes were planted with black varieties, and the wine, spilling over onto the emperor's flowing beard, left some red stains. Madame Charlemagne, concerned for her husband's dignity, complained about his love of the wine. To keep the peace he had the slopes dug up and replanted with white varieties. In doing so he could satisfy his fondness for the wine without staining his mane or incurring his wife's reproaches."

To me such elaborate myths seem unnecessary, given the quality of the wines and the extraordinary continuity which marks this commune. The Pavelot family, for example, have been able to trace ancestors in Corton as far back as the year 1111. Yet it took them eight centuries to become landowners: they bought their first vines in 1930. And, more grandly, the vineyard owned by Charlemagne before he presented it to the Church was held, until his death in 1969, by René Bonneau du Martray, the direct descendant of Nicolas Rolin, most flamboyant of ducal chancellors.

Harvest-time at Aloxe-Corton: hard, unglamorous work. Rain is always possible, the weather likely to be cold.

CHAPTER THREE

BEAUNE MEANS BUSINESS

THE HEART OF BEAUNE IS SURROUNDED BY MEDIEVAL WALLS, STILL STANDING, STILL HOUSING THE

CELLARS OF MANY OF THE HUNDREDS OF MERCHANTS WHO MAKE THIS THE MOST WINE-ORIENTED TOWN IN

THE WORLD. AT THEIR BEST THESE FIRMS, SOME OF WHICH DATE BACK TO THE 18TH CENTURY, PROVIDE A

GUARANTEE OF QUALITY OF THE WINES THAT THEY MAKE OR THAT THEY BUY FROM GROWERS — THOUGH THE

LESS SCRUPULOUS ARE LARGELY RESPONSIBLE FOR THE UNRELIABILITY OF MANY OF THE REGION'S WINES.

BEAUNE ALSO PLAYS HOST TO THE MOST PUBLICIZED OCCASION IN THE BURGUNDIAN YEAR: THE ANNUAL

AUCTION OF WINES FROM THE ESTATES OF THE HOSPICES DE BEAUNE, THE TOWN'S HISTORIC

HOSPITAL, HELD EVERY NOVEMBER IN THE MAGNIFICENT 15TH-CENTURY HÔTEL-DIEU. THE SALE, AN EVENT

THAT IN ITS INTRICACIES RESEMBLES A GAME OF CRICKET RATHER THAN A NORMAL AUCTION, IS NO MERE

RELIC — THE PRICES THAT THE WINES FETCH PROVIDE AN INVALUABLE GUIDE TO THE MARKET AS A WHOLE.

60 It is a curious experience to attend a press conference on the wines of Burgundy. The words are familiar: "Our prices have not risen as far as those of our competitors ... but we need to make sure that our wines are worthy of the name of Burgundy." But the setting is a 15th-century hall within the Hôtel-Dieu, a complex rightly described by the guidebooks as "a marvel of Burgundian-Flemish art". To emphasize the former close connection of Burgundy with Flanders, the Hôtel-Dieu also houses Rogier van der Weyden's polyptych, *The Last Judgment*. The hall is all the more striking because, although its ceiling is magnificently decorated, the sides are lined with beds in which, for centuries, the sick and the old of Beaune were housed. But then the Hôtel-Dieu is like that: a masterpiece that is rather taken for granted by the town it serves. While tourists come to gape at its splendours, to the inhabitants of Beaune it is – refreshingly unlike similar monuments in other towns – simply part of their daily life.

The building itself is a sprawling monument to Nicolas Rolin, former chancellor to the Duchy, an enormously rich man who gained immortality by returning to the poor of Beaune some of the money he had previously extracted from them. For centuries, until a new facility was opened on the outskirts of the town in 1971, "God's House" was the town's hospital and even today part of it is given over to a geriatric nursing home.

The Hôtel-Dieu is by no means Beaune's only historic monument. There are dozens of old houses and streets concentrated within the town walls. One example is the mansion formerly occupied by the dukes of Burgundy, which houses a "living museum" of Burgundian wine and winemaking – France's first museum of this type when it was established in 1946.

An 18th-century work by the French artist Souville shows an apothecary brewing up a mysterious potion in his pharmacy within the Hôtel-Dieu at Beaune.

C. MORELOT
APOTHIC
AIRE·NÉ·LE·
17 FEUVRIER
1719

C. Souville P. 1761.

Although Beaune has sprawled far beyond its walled centre, it remains the most purely wine-oriented town in the world. As such, it attracts millions of wine tourists. They are catered for by more than a hundred restaurants, many concentrating on such local dishes as *escargots*, as well as dozens of establishments selling wine, ranging from modest shops (though on closer inspection the prices are anything but modest) to enormous cellars owned by local merchants.

This being Burgundy, proper attention is paid to food – in the shops and more particularly the market. "It is a town of greedy eaters," writes Anthony Hanson, "the Saturday-morning market yielding Cîteaux cheeses, corn-coloured Bresse chickens, perhaps a haunch of young wild boar (the blood supplied separately, no extra charge, in a jam jar). The inhabitants will tell you how to

Tomatoes and summer flowers on their way to one of Beaune's delightful markets.

choose your butcher, this one for pork, that one for veal, another for chickens. In Beaune, the weather is predicted by feeling the bread: *le pain est mou, il va pleuvoir* [the bread is soft, it's going to rain]."

Historically, Beaune was the great rival to Dijon, 50 kilometres to the north, housing the Valois dukes of Burgundy until 1443 and defending Burgundy's independence against the French invaders far more obstinately than Dijon (a stand that cost the town dearly, as it did another hold-out, Chassagne-Montrachet). But Beaune lost out: the same size as Dijon at the beginning of the 19th century, within a hundred years it was a mere fifth of the size. Nevertheless, it is still a crossroads, reachable by relatively uncrowded motorways, not only from much of northern France but also from Switzerland, Germany and the Low Countries. And it remains the vinous capital of the historic Duchy of Burgundy.

The heart of the town, less than a kilometre across, is enclosed by ramparts dating back to the 15th and 16th

64 centuries. They're still mostly intact and over the ages have acquired a homely look, covered with domestic creepers, and with immaculate private gardens and tennis courts nestling beneath them. On each of the four corners of the town there is a mighty bastion, each of which has a story to tell. By some quirk of fate (or is it because the *genius loci* of the town is so strong that any building, built for whatever purpose, is automatically suitable for making and storing wine?), the 15th-century Bastion de l'Oratoire, a four-storey look-out tower, with its walls up to 8 metres thick, makes an admirable headquarters for one of the town's oldest wine firms, Chanson. Owned until recently by the Marion-Chanson family, Chanson was one of the merchants known as the "Big Five" (the others being Jadot, Drouhin, Bouchard Père et Fils and Latour). As in an ultra-modern winery, the two entrances are at different levels, enabling the wine to arrive at what

was the top of the ramparts, and to descend floor by floor as it ages until it departs by lorry at street level. Chanson is not the only firm to choose an historic base — for a long time the cellars of another major merchant, Jaffelin, were housed in the Roman *castrum*, Beaune's earliest settlement.

The merchants arrived in two waves. First came the houses that specialized in the *roulage* of wines to the Low Countries, generally in return for textiles – hence the natural connection between the two trades (a pattern found to an even greater extent in Champagne). As so often in the history of Burgundy, these merchants are not merely of antiquarian interest. Champy, the oldest, founded in

ABOVE: *Only light – and, apparently, old-fashioned – lorries allowed on one of Burgundy's many winding roads.* RIGHT: *In the autumn even the Virginia creeper turns purple.*

1720, is taking on a new lease of life. The second wave of firms, based on estates owned by the local bourgeoisie, were founded during the latter half of the 18th century. They included Patriarche and the predecessors of Louis Jadot. Other merchants, like Claude Morey from Nuits, would acquire a scattering of vines in as many famous vineyards as they could afford. One local man, Claude Jobert, in the words of a contemporary, "borrowed up to the hilt but bought everything he could" – including much of the Clos de Bèze. All these merchants sold the wines far more actively than had their ecclesiastical predecessors.

Jules Ouvrard was one of those fabled wheeler-dealers who emerge from every uprising. Heir to the empire of a financier father, he snapped up a number of properties, including the Clos de Vougeot, after the restoration of the monarchy in 1815. But more typical, because more local, and longer-lasting, were the Bouchards. They were already well established as merchants before 1789, and thus in an excellent position to take advantage of the sale of monastic properties. Nothing could better symbolize the transition than their famous vineyard, Vigne de l'Enfant Jésus at Beaune-Grèves, which had been the property of the Carmelite nuns of Beaune.

The Bouchards and their brethren were helped by the suppression of the customs barriers between Burgundy and its traditional trading partners in the Rhineland and the Low Countries. A further boost came from the

LEFT: *Franz Hals' portrayal of serious Dutch trencherpersons, who invariably drank the wine of Burgundy – their former suzerain.* ABOVE: *Some cellars – notably those of Bouchard Père et Fils – contain thousands of wine bottles dating back to the 19th century.*

68 development of France's railway network, countering once and for all Burgundy's historic inaccessibility. Later free-trade treaties negotiated by Napoleon III (above all that with Britain) were also of great benefit.

Unfortunately, too many of the merchants became lazy, their philosophy, as Hanson puts it, that "Beaune wines be designed principally never to offend anyone." It is also unfortunate that the firms discourage visitors from inspecting Beaune's vineyards, which stretch in a magnificent bowl above the town. None has Grand Cru status but all can produce smooth, easy- and early-drinking wines (not only the reds – the whites are too often overlooked), and can be very good value – especially those from Savigny-lès-Beaune, up the hill toward Corton.

After the Second World War, the merchants' position was undermined by Americans such as Alexis Lichine. Lichine terrified them, because he insisted on dealing directly with the growers. Unable to match his prices and no longer able to lay their hands on the wines made by some of the best growers, many of the merchants found it more sensible to buy land again as their forefathers had done. Their finances, sound enough in the 1950s and 1960s, were dealt a severe blow by the Middle East oil crisis of 1973, which led to a sharp reduction in their purchases of the finer wines, thus providing an even greater opportunity – indeed a need – for growers to sell their wines directly.

The complexity of the relationships between growers and merchants concealed an underlying complacency resulting from the continuing willingness of the world to pay for wines labelled "Burgundy" regardless of quality. But the average quality of the wines has been helped by the increasing acreage now owned, managed or leased by competent growers or merchants, and by the takeover of a number of major firms by outsiders. In the 1980s and

ABOVE: *The cellars of Louis Jadot, one of Beaune's finest merchants.* BELOW: *Some of the firm's most venerable bottles.*

1990s, Louis Jadot was bought by its American importers, Drouhin by a Japanese importer, Chanson by Bollinger and Bouchard Père et Fils by Joseph Henriot, inheritor of a well-respected family estate in Champagne and the former managing director of Veuve Clicquot. All these newcomers can bring in more capital than is available to the locals. Indeed, of the "Big Five" only Louis Latour remains in family hands.

Henriot made dramatic changes after a purchase which, including vineyards bought from the Ropiteau family, added up to more than 130 hectares – the biggest holding on the Côte d'Or, and twice the size of the estate owned by the Hospice de Beaune. The fact that he had to make these changes shows the neglect to which insufficient investment can lead. Vines needed replacing (in Ropiteau's case there were rows of white grapes

LEFT AND RIGHT: *The temples of wine that house the oldest bottles have suitably ecclesiastical entrances.*

scattered through some of the best red vineyards) and above all the winery had to be re-equipped. The essential winemaking tool in Burgundy is a mass of small vats, able to cope with the tiny quantities normal in the finest vineyards. Previously – and only too typically of the region's many family-owned firms (and estates, for that matter) – the juice from many different plots was fermented together. Until the takeover all the Meursaults owned by Ropiteau were sold as a single wine – now they are separated into a dozen or more. Not having enough vats meant that the wines were fermented for far too short a time, in order to make way for the next batch of grapes. The potential for such congestion has been exacerbated by global warming, which now means that the harvest can last little more than a fortnight, a third of the previous time. Moreover, only new capital can ensure an adequate supply of new casks, to give the winemaker more freedom to choose how much wood, and of what age, he or she should use.

72 The strengths and weaknesses of the Burgundian tradition are perhaps epitomized by the sale of wines from the estates owned by the Hospices de Beaune. For me, this – surely the weirdest event in the world of wine – resembles nothing so much as a Burgundian cricket match: the little that seems to happen is of passionate interest to those involved and to aficionados of the game, but is interminably boring to an outsider. Since the tradition was finally established in 1959, it has been held every year on the third Sunday of November, and involves the auctioning for charity of the finest wines produced from the 61 hectares of vines owned by the Hospices – almost exclusively from its Premier and Grand Cru vineyards

scattered the length and breadth of the Côte d'Or. Many of these vineyards were given to the Hospices by generous benefactors. Nicolas Rolin was the first donor, but there have been dozens throughout the centuries – the latest being someone who turned up at the office of the director of the Hospices a few years ago and explained that his wife and children were taken care of and would they like 23 hectares of vines?

ABOVE: *Burning the insides of casks prevents the wine from becoming too tannic.* RIGHT: *The members of the Brotherhood of St Michael in Beaune from 1713 to 1772 – master coopers all, and some, like the Champys, Naudins and Gillots on the list, ancestors of winemakers still famous in Burgundy today.*

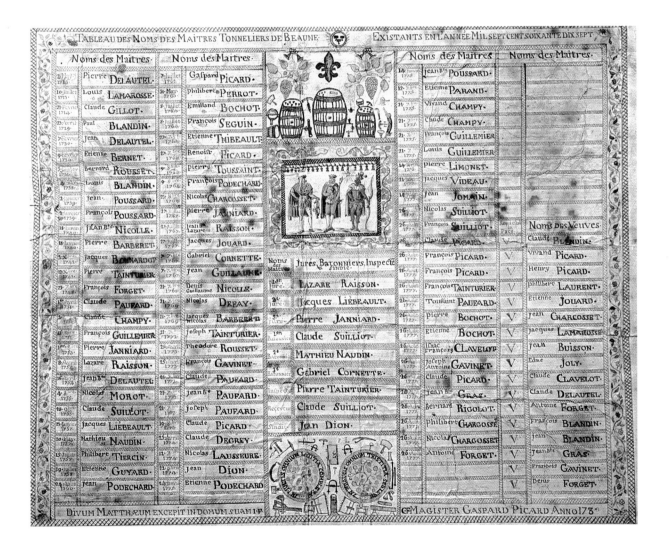

At the auction the wines are sold in batches of five or more *pièces* – the Burgundian cask holding 228 litres, or around 300 bottles. The proceeds of the sales have risen, irregularly, from 1.4 million francs in the mid-1960s to 34.6 million in 2000, though 2001 showed a drop of more than a fifth. The money used to go to the maintenance of the hospital, but now pays for new buildings, equipment and other worthy causes, including a home in which down-and-outs are restored to a life in the community.

The sale is held in the old – but still functioning – market hall within the Hôtel-Dieu, and only registered merchants can bid. But few, if any, of them are bidding purely or even mainly for themselves – they will be representing a whole host of other eager buyers. In 2001 these ranged from well-known French restaurants to individual Americans, and hotels from as far afield as

FAR LEFT AND LEFT: *Casks like these, at more than £300 (US $450) apiece, represent an enormous investment.*

Japan and Russia. The bidding process is long and tortuous – which is where the cricketing analogy comes in. The (professional) auctioneer asks for bids but the fate of the wine is decided only after two "candles" have been lit and their light has died down without any further bid. (It seemed to me that the person responsible for lighting the candles, which are in fact merely wicks, could have speeded up the process if he had wished.) As a result, the sale of about 150 lots, the work of an hour at a normal auction, can last up to four and a half hours – the fact that it doesn't start until everyone has enjoyed a lengthy Sunday lunch does nothing to accelerate proceedings.

The director of the Hospices proposed to adopt a more sensible and more modern procedure, but the idea was rejected out of hand by the merchants – although in 2001 the bidding was in euros rather than francs. The participants enjoy the wheeling and dealing which occupies the minutes between the bids, including whispered requests to leading bidders to act as underwriters to ensure that none of the lots is sold below a reasonable price. The publicity attached to any wine from the sale ensures that the lots go for between three and four times what they would fetch without the Hospices label. Nevertheless, the prices provide a rough indication of year-on-year market trends.

In the past, the quality of the lots varied wildly, and in 1993, in particular, the wines were not up to snuff. But the arrival of a new director brought major changes. The individual *vignerons* ceased to have total control of the plots they cultivated and, crucially, the winemaking was moved to spacious new premises next to the new hospital. Even then the winemaker, André Porcheret, went in for short fermentation times so that the wines should be forward enough to be tastable a few weeks later. In 2001, partly because his successor had allowed the wines to develop their own character rather than imposing a "house style" on them, prices varied wildly according to quality.

It is difficult to judge fine wines a mere couple of months after the harvest, especially those that benefit from long fermentation times. Within a few months of the sale, the wines are taken away by the buyers and there is no guarantee that they will be properly looked after to ensure that they remain worthy of the name of the Hospices – or of Burgundy as a whole. Yet the idea of waiting a few months, let alone selling wines from the previous vintage, is simply unthinkable. But, given the continuing international success of the sale, why should the Burgundians take positive steps to improve quality? Unfortunately, this question still applies, though to a far lesser extent than it did a few years ago, throughout the finer communes of the Côte d'Or.

The steep roofs of the 15th-century Hospices de Beaune typify the architecture of the period.

CHAPTER FOUR

THE SACRED STONES OF MONTRACHET

JUST SOUTH OF BEAUNE COME TWO LITTLE VILLAGES THAT VIVIDLY ILLUSTRATE THE DIVERSITY OF THE REGION'S RED WINES. WHILE THE REDS FROM POMMARD ARE RELATIVELY HARD (LIKE THOSE FROM GEVREY-CHAMBERTIN SOUTH OF DIJON), THOSE FROM ITS SOUTHERN NEIGHBOUR VOLNAY ARE SOFT AND ELEGANT. BUT THE GREATEST GLORIES OF THE SLOPES ARE THE WHITE WINES. THEY COME FROM MEURSAULT, SCENE OF THE PAULÉE WHERE THE GROWERS GATHER EVERY NOVEMBER TO COMPARE WINES, AND FROM CHASSAGNE-MONTRACHET AND PULIGNY-MONTRACHET, TWIN VILLAGES WHOSE INHABITANTS DISTRUST EACH OTHER WITH A FORCE INCOMPREHENSIBLE TO THOSE NOT FULLY AU FAIT WITH RURAL FRANCE. IT IS CHASSAGNE WHICH HOUSES LE MONTRACHET, THE VINEYARD OF LESS THAN TEN HECTARES THAT PRODUCES THE WORLD'S FINEST CHARDONNAY, A MIRACLE OF BALANCE AND AROMATIC DELIGHT.

Pommard is only a few kilometres south of Beaune; yet, such is the patchwork-quiltishness of Burgundy that the slopes above the compact little village produce wines completely different from those of its larger neighbour. The wines, writes Anthony Hanson, "... have an old reputation for ageing and travelling well. They are described as solid, well-constructed wines of deep colour, comparable to good Cortons or Gevrey-Chambertins in their need to be laid away to soften up." Unfortunately, the name is so easy to remember, the wines so type-cast over the ages, that they have been only too easy to sell, "lulling growers into a false sense of security," as Hanson puts it, and removing the impetus to produce wines that are out of the ordinary. In the past Pommard suffered badly from frauds, with any powerful and deeply coloured wine pretending to its name.

Even normally peaceable Pommard can be dramatic in the right — or rather the wrong — weather.

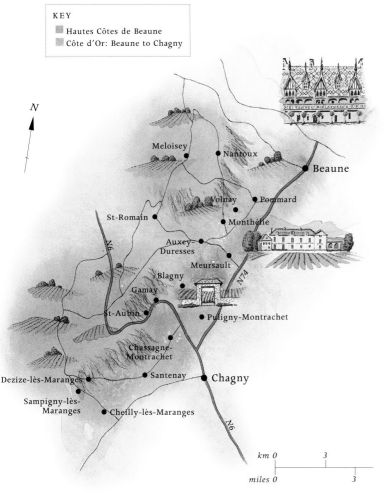

KEY

▦ Hautes Côtes de Beaune

▦ Côte d'Or: Beaune to Chagny

N

Meloisey

Nantoux

Beaune

Volnay · Pommard

St-Romain

Monthélie

Auxey-
Duresses

Meursault

Blagny

Gamay

St-Aubin

Puligny-Montrachet

Chassagne-
Montrachet

Dezize-lès-Maranges

Santenay · Chagny

Sampigny-lès-
Maranges

Cheilly-lès-Maranges

N6

N74

N6

km 0   3

miles 0   3

Fortunately, there are a handful of inspired winemakers in the village, like Jean-Marc Boillot and, straddling Pommard and Volnay, the de Montille family. Indeed, the wines from the single hectare of vines attached to the Château de Pommard are now being made by Étienne de Montille, whose father, Hubert, not only presided over a thriving law practice but also produced exemplary wines that brought out the individual qualities of each of his holdings.

Just south of Pommard lies Volnay. The contrast between the wines of the two communes is a perfect demonstration that the historic division between the Côte de Beaune and the Côte de Nuits has no bearing on the character of their wines. For, just as Pommard can best be compared to Chambertin, so Volnay is most like Vosne-Romanée or Chambolle-Musigny. Jean-François Bazin describes Volnay as "feminine", and certainly it is softer, silkier than Pommard. The village itself shows to perfection the traditional layout of a Burgundian

82 vineyard. The Premiers Crus are in the middle of the slope, on both sides of the *route des vins*. Some of them, most obviously the Caillerets, at the heart of the vineyard, could have claimed the title of Grand Cru, but in the 1930s the Marquis d'Angerville made it a point of honour not to claim the title for his own eminently deserving vineyard in Volnay. The Premiers Crus form the central slice of bread in a double-decker sandwich. The inner layer of communal wines cluster round them and there are outer layers both high up on the slopes (around 275 metres above sea level) and below the village. Toward, and even beyond, the main road is another slice of vineyard allowed only to call its wines *bourgogne rouge*.

Volnay's history, too, is classic Burgundy. Its vineyards were owned at one time or another by abbeys, the Knights of Malta, and various dukes of Burgundy and kings of France. The wine was a favourite of Louis XIV and was served at the coronation of his great-grandson Louis XV, who, however, was only five at the time and so probably too young to appreciate its velvety qualities. In the 1930s the leading figure in the commune, the late Marquis d'Angerville, pioneered the rigorous application of Appellation d'Origine Contrôlée regulations. The result was that the local merchants, clearly an unscrupulous lot, closed ranks against him and he was forced (to his great advantage – albeit only in the long term) into bottling and selling his wines himself, a highly unusual practice at the time.

In the Burgundian fashion, the vineyards of Volnay mingle with those of Meursault, which produce one of the best-known of white wines, buttery with a touch of solid oatmeal, generally richer and thus easier to drink young than its southern neighbours. The land is so valuable that when the late André Boisseaux bought the Château de Meursault estate in 1973, he pulled down a number of houses and planted vines in their place – as

The huddled houses of Volnay lit up by the evening sun.

Bazin says, making them the only vines in the world with telephone and main sewerage. The village is home to one of the great occasions in the Burgundian calendar, the Paulée, a long, but not interminable, feast held the Monday after the sale at the Hospices de Beaune (see pp.72–7) and forming the last, and most informal (and thus most agreeable), stage in the "Trois Glorieuses". The name *Paulée* has been variously attributed to *poêlée* (a casserole), people standing *épaule à épaule* (shoulder to shoulder) or *paulier* (the tithe-collector). The event dates back to 1923 when Jules Lafon – whose family's vineyards still produce some of the best wines in the commune – invited friends to a harvest supper. The next year they were joined by another major local owner, Jacques Prieur, and his friends, and in the 1930s they organized the Paulée as the white-wine equivalent of the dinner held by the Chevaliers du Tastevin at the Clos de Vougeot, complete with the first literary prize (a hundred bottles of Meursault) for books on wine – a classic piece of pioneering Burgundian promotionalism.

The Paulée is a friendly but professional affair with the *vignerons* bringing sample bottles to be tasted and compared with those of their neighbours. This is a habit normal in the New World but startlingly innovative in the Burgundy of the 1930s and still unusual – even the wines tasted with a view to being served at the Clos de Vougeot dinners are still strictly anonymous. The Paulée has done more to ensure that Meursault's wines are generally of a high standard than all the decrees issued by the French government over the past 70 years.

The production of the region's finest wines is concentrated in the hands of a relatively small number of families, each generation suffused with the responsibility of taking on their parents' precious vines – a

ABOVE: *Meursault at dawn with the vines nuzzling up to the village.* BELOW: *Les Pucelles, a classic walled Premier Cru in Puligny-Montrachet, complete with formal stone gate.*

charge that weighs all the heavier now that the children will almost certainly have enjoyed a proper vinous education at a technical high school. But the lines of inheritance can be complicated. For me it is the two great white-wine communes south of Meursault – Puligny-Montrachet and Chassagne-Montrachet – that best illustrate this tangle. For example, in Chassagne you have Laurence Fontaine-Gagnard, the daughter of Jacques Gagnard-Delagrange and granddaughter of Edmond Delagrange-Bachelet. Her sister is Claudine Blain-Gagnard. Each of the four has a quite distinct estate.

The two villages also demonstrate the historic swing between white and red wines. It can be seen most clearly in Chassagne-Montrachet: today's wine snobs look askance at the reds produced there, seeing them as intruders in a white stronghold. But in 1855 Dr Lavalle, scientist and author, noted that the red wines from Puligny, today a commune of total white purity, were as highly valued as anything from any other part of the

Côte de Beaune. Not surprisingly, when I spoke to him Jacques Gagnard-Delagrange was much more interested in discussing the delicious red wines of Chassagne, and, in particular, why they were relatively undervalued, especially as they used to sell more easily than the whites. Indeed, twenty-five years ago three-fifths of the commune was planted in Pinot as against two-fifths in Chardonnay, proportions now completely reversed. Although the reds are more reliable, the whites have the unfair advantage of all being planted in the best spots, so the undervaluation looks likely to continue.

Of course, there are further contrasts between Chassagne and Puligny, apart from the distinctions between their *terroirs*. Socially, they have always lived at arm's length – symbolically there is a valley between

LEFT: *The village of St-Romain. Note the very similar roofs – and the very different chimneys.* RIGHT: *An ancient, almost Celtic, cross in Puligny-Montrachet.*

88 them. Typically, although there are seven families called Chavy in Puligny, none of them will admit to any relationship with families of the same name in Chassagne. Moreover, the wines from Puligny are usually put on the market earlier than those from Chassagne, because the water-table is so high that it is impossible to dig cellars there. As a result the wines have to be stored at ground level. The (invariably white) wines from Puligny are so easy to sell that some growers allow their vines to over-produce, especially those who sell their production as juice to be fermented elsewhere, and who therefore have no interest in its quality. By contrast, recent white wines from Chassagne have often proved more subtle and distinctive. The wine writer Oz Clarke's contrast, "Puligny-Montrachet, structured, savoury and tight; Chassagne-Montrachet, nuttier," seems to me pretty fair.

In his remarkable book on Puligny, Simon Loftus remarks that its wines "... tend to complexity, the latter [from Chassagne] to pungency. Puligny, for better or worse, has been afflicted by civilization. Chassagne maintains a stronger, less refined sense of peasant vigour." Chassagne has fewer Grands and Premiers Crus and depends far more on wine than its neighbour, which has arable land below to cultivate in times when the wine is selling badly (as it did until well after 1945, a fact difficult to understand today).

Not surprisingly, both villages helped to promote their wines by suffixing Montrachet – their most famous vineyard – to their names. Like its red equivalent, Romanée-Conti, this fabulous wine – from a vineyard four times the size but divided among a dozen owners – first came to prominence in the 18th century.

In 1728 the learned *abbé* Claude Arnoux declared that Montrachet "... produces the most remarkable and delicious white wine in France ... this wine has qualities

The apparently similar vines on each side of this road in Puligny-Montrachet can yield grapes worth very different sums.

of softness which neither the French nor the Latin language can express ... I have drunk it six or seven times and can witness to its delicacy." But even then, as he said, "You must buy it in advance since it's always sold before the harvest." A century later Cyrus Redding wrote that the wine "... is remarked in good years for its fineness, lightness, bouquet and exquisite delicacy, having spirit without too great dryness, and a luscious taste without cloying." Nothing much has changed since then.

Unlike Romanée-Conti, which is a high altar surrounded by acolyte vineyards, Le Montrachet (meaning, fittingly, "the stony hill") is well up the slopes, with only Chevalier-Montrachet above it. The three other Grands Crus entitled to use the name Montrachet are below. Simon Loftus provides a more scientific analysis of the distinctions between the vineyard of Le Montrachet

Harvesting is hard work – each hod of grapes can weigh more than 40 kilograms.

itself and its satellites. He concentrates on the mix of the soils with the clay overlying the limestone. Clay particles, he points out, "... account for 50 per cent of the soil in Bâtard-Montrachet, about 35 per cent in Montrachet and only about 20 per cent in Chevalier: an arithmetic progression which almost exactly expressed the contrast between the power of Bâtard, at the bottom of the hill, and the finesse of Chevalier (at the top) with Montrachet itself the perfect synthesis between the two." The same sense of balance applies to the slope – less steep than Montrachet in Bâtard, greater than Montrachet in Chevalier. But all the vineyards face roughly south-east, with the scrub at the top of the hill breaking the force of the cold west winds – as vital a point in Burgundy as it is in Champagne, which lies even further north.

In the past there were fewer direct sales from Puligny than from many other famous communes, because the height of the water-table made small-scale winemaking so difficult. But over the past 80 years, the Leflaive

92 family has proved to be the exception to this rule, and indeed many others. Not only have they acquired an enviable world-wide reputation for their wines, but they are now repeating the transition made in the 18th and 19th centuries by the Bouchards and their like, from vineyard owners to merchants in their own right, relying not only on the sacred names of the plots they hold but also on the family's own name.

There have always been Leflaives in the region – well, if not always, then at least since 1580 when a certain Marc Le Flayve is recorded as living in Cissey. In 1779 the second of five generations of Leflaives, all called Claude, married a girl from Puligny, one Anne Barraut. His great-grandson was more adventurous, calling his son Claude-Joseph, who called his son simply Joseph. Joseph inherited a mere two hectares of vines, but bequeathed a whole estate to his children. He was a remarkable person – a brilliant student who became one of the first graduates of France's leading engineering school, the Polytechnique, to have come from a humble background. He went on to be a maritime engineer and helped build the first French submarine. He retired early and in 1926 returned to Puligny, blazing a trail as the first of many Burgundians to come home to till the family plot after a distinguished career in the wider world. A fervent believer in the vineyard at a time of widespread despair, he had already bought another 25 hectares of vines as well as the buildings in Puligny that are now used for making and storing its wine. As an often absentee owner at first – and as a good manager – he entrusted the wine-making largely to another brilliant local, François Virot, a leading authority on viticulture. Leflaive and Virot uprooted the Aligoté and Gamay that had found their way even into Puligny as a result of the post-phylloxera depression, and planted Chardonnay.

It was Joseph's youngest son, Vincent, who made the reputation of the estate's wines in the decades after 1945. He was supported by his brother, Joseph (who, in keeping with the family tradition, also held down a responsible job in Paris). Vincent's greatest triumph came in 1991 when he was able to buy a tiny slice of Montrachet itself, albeit a mere couple of *ouvrées*. It was, as Loftus points out, "... the first time for more than two hundred years that anyone in Puligny has been able to lay claim to a portion of that 'stony hill.'" By contrast, Bâtard-Montrachet has always been a democratic vineyard. As early as the middle of the 19th century the average holding there was a mere three *ouvrées*, and today the biggest slice is less than a hectare, most covering a mere 15 ares (an are is a hundredth of a hectare).

The Leflaive family tradition is being maintained by Vincent's daughter, Anne-Claude, a trained oenologist, who, like that other formidable Burgundian lady, Lalou Bize-Leroy, has gone beyond the ecological grape-growing essential in so long-established and chemical-

The dramatically differing colours of the autumnal vines.

drenched a vineyard as Burgundy. Both have taken the next step: producing wines through bio-dynamic methods – a process fraught with problems in difficult years, but resulting in wines of extraordinary concentration (and, in the case of Madame Bize-Leroy, of extraordinary price as well). Eighteen years ago, after a restless period spent in show-business, Anne-Claude's cousin, Olivier, set up on his own. He has developed his business with the help of a distinguished winemaker, Franck Grux, and by systematically creating relationships with many growers, advising them and buying their grapes or juice to produce wines worthy of the family name.

Chassagne-Montrachet is the last bastion of the Côte d'Or before the *route des vins* curves up the combe and back round toward Auxey-Duresses. The area bounded by Auxey, Volnay and Meursault is known locally as a sacred triangle – the "sanctuary of Celtic wine," in Bazin's words. In the middle of the triangle, up the hill behind Volnay and Pommard, lies Monthélie. This small village is totally devoted to vines – producing wines which traditionally are sold at a mere three-quarters of the prices of those from the better-known communes below, and therefore can be better value. But it has to be said that the last commune in the Côte d'Or, Santenay, is included in the Côte d'Or rather than the Côte Chalonnaise because of administrative convenience rather than vinous quality.

LEFT: *A peaceful evening in the little village of Monthélie.*
OVERLEAF: *In the distance, Volnay almost disappears in the mists of autumn.*

CHAPTER FIVE

THE CHALLENGERS

OFTEN BURGUNDY HAS BEEN DEFINED TOO NARROWLY, EXCLUDING THREE SUB-REGIONS CAPABLE OF PRO-

DUCING DELICIOUS WINES. ABOVE THE CÔTE D'OR LIE THE HAUTES CÔTES — WILD, BEAUTIFUL, ROLLING,

WINDSWEPT COUNTRYSIDE. THANKS TO GLOBAL WARMING, THE GRAPES FROM THE VINEYARDS OF THE

HAUTES CÔTES NOW RIPEN EARLIER, AND MORE RELIABLY, THAN BEFORE TO PRODUCE THE BEST-VALUE

WINES IN THE WHOLE REGION. BUT BOUZERON, RULLY, MERCUREY, GIVRY AND MONTAGNY, THE FIVE VIL-

LAGES OF THE CÔTE CHALONNAISE, TO THE SOUTH OF THE CÔTE D'OR, PROVIDE STIFF COMPETITION —

ABOVE ALL, THE BEST WHITE WINES FROM RULLY AND THE FINEST REDS FROM A SUNNY BOWL OF VINES IN

MERCUREY. AND THERE'S ONE JOKER IN THE PACK: THE CRISPLY AROMATIC WHITE WINE OF BOUZERON,

MADE FROM THE ALIGOTÉ GRAPE. EVEN MORE FIERCE COMPETITION COMES FROM THE MÂCONNAIS,

AROUND THE TOWN THAT GIVES THE REGION ITS NAME, WHOSE BEST WHITE WINES, SUCH AS THOSE OF

POUILLY-FUISSÉ, ARE CRISP AND DELICIOUSLY FRUITY — INDEED, UNIQUE.

The growers and merchants on the Côte d'Or are often accused of complacency, but the less well-placed wine communities – above the Côte d'Or on the "Hautes Côtes", to the south on the Côte Chalonnaise, and further south in the Mâconnais – are hungry, and willing to produce increasingly impressive wines far more reasonably than their more prestigious neighbours.

The contrast is most obvious in the Hautes Côtes, the empty, beautiful, windswept slopes above the Côte d'Or. Indeed, whenever I visit the Hautes Côtes I leave my heart in its dozens of little villages. They are totally different from the Côte d'Or, yet so near. A mere 8 kilometres above the dusty bustle of Nuits-St-Georges you

---

RIGHT: *One of the little huts, the* maisons de quatre heures *("four o'clock houses") as they're called in Burgundy, which shelter the vineyard workers – and give them somewhere to take their afternoon break.* FAR RIGHT: *In Burgundy the vines are packed closely together, with up to 10,000 on every hectare.*

are in another world, the valleys are steeper, the hand of man less obtrusive, his artefacts blending with the hilly slopes, green, not only with vines, which occupy only a minority of the land, but also with the pasture and hedgerows absent from viticulturally more glorious spots. To complete the picture there are fruit trees, and raspberry and blackcurrant bushes – as well as the occasional pig or cow.

The grapes ripen only where the slopes are tilted favourably toward the east, or even better the south-east or south, to catch every possible ray of the sun. Yet in geographical, even geological, terms, the Hautes Côtes are only a continuation of the Côte d'Or – the soils are the same Jurassic-limestone mix as found below. Indeed, in some ways the climate is even more suitable for the quirky demands of the Pinot than that of the Côte itself. It may be cooler, but it is sunnier – because of a temperature inversion the slopes below suffer from mists and the cool air forms above.

Today this usually despised region is being revived: winemakers are steadily reclaiming the old vineyards, deducing from piles of stones removed from the patch in earlier attempts to create a vineyard that once upon a time there had been vines there. The reason for the rebirth is very simple. Growers in the two separate vineyards, the Hautes Côtes de Nuits and the Hautes Côtes de Beaune, have benefited recently from global warming. This means that the harvest is now three weeks earlier than it was only a couple of decades ago when the growers' children were regularly taken out of school for a fortnight in mid- or late October to help with picking. Today the wines from the Hautes Côtes are still deceptively light in colour, but many of the best have an excellent depth, length and richness.

The history, as well as the geology, of the Hautes

This cross marks the entrance to the Domaine de la Romanée-Conti, the finest vineyard in Burgundy. The estate is undertaking the restoration of the abbey of St Vivant on the Hautes Côtes.

Côtes is connected to that of the Côte d'Or, with the Church playing a vital role. The abbey of St Vivant, high above the vineyards of the Côte d'Or, was founded at the end of the ninth century by monks from what is now Normandy fleeing the Norman invaders. The monks chose to store within the precincts of the abbey the wine that they made from all its vineyards, including Romanée-St-Vivant, to ensure that it would be safe. The Domaine de la Romanée-Conti (see pp.54–5), owner of Romanée-St-Vivant, is now restoring the abbey. And the region's own wines were once famous. Medieval kings served wines from Meloisey, one of the most picturesque of the villages nestling in the high valleys, and the dukes of Burgundy had a cellar there. What's more, in the 18th century, the wines of a neighbouring commune, Nantoux, were rated above those of Pommard.

The region's decline started with the Revolution, and with the consequent end to the discipline first imposed four hundred years earlier by Duke Philip the Bold, who forbade the planting of that over-prolific variety, the Gamay. But even a century ago there were five times as many vines as there are now. The Gamay – and the hybrids planted before and after the Second World War – were the undoing of the region's reputation, even though the authorities insisted that only wines made from Pinot Noir be granted an *appellation*, and then only one with a clumsy and unappealing name: Bourgogne des Côteaux des Beaunois or Bourgogne des Côteaux des Nuitons.

The result was despair, and neglect of vineyards. If the growers did replant they preferred enormously productive hybrids rather than the unpredictable rewards from the Pinot. Not surprisingly, in the first part of the 20th century the young fled in droves to the towns and the population halved. But, ironically, the renaissance started with the Second World War, when there was a demand for wine of any sort, and the flight to the towns was halted by wartime restrictions on travel.

The restoration of the vineyard was largely down to an unjustly forgotten figure, the late Étienne Kayser. At the end of the War he was the schoolmaster at Meloisey, "the father-confessor to the village, the lay priest," he once told me. "I was teaching between twenty and forty children of all ages from five to thirteen. When their parents first asked me for advice I didn't know what to tell them. To begin with, I advised them to return to the region's old speciality – fruit trees."

The cooperative he formed was revolutionary (and not only in Burgundian terms), because it grouped growers from more than one commune – today the Hautes Côtes de Beaune and the Hautes Côtes de Nuits have a joint *syndicat*. When Kayser asked them what varieties they were growing, more often than not they told him Gamay. He advised them to replant, and only with Pinot Noir, and to learn to vinify properly – the Institut

---

Where vines are not profitable, they are replaced by sunflowers whose oil is much prized in these health-conscious days.

Oenologique at Beaune proved generous with guidance. But above all the wines had to be saleable. As early as 1951 he set up a communal tasting, through the "friends of the wines of the Hautes Côtes". Lacking the self-assurance of the growers below, the Hautes Côtes were going to ensure from the first that their wines would at least be properly made.

Kayser also understood the need for proper marketing. The best wines were awarded a "Prix d'Excellence" and good wines were all given a "Diplôme des Vins des Hautes Côtes". He even organized annual picnics ("what a lot of work that was!"), first at the historic town of La Rochepot, then in 1953 at Mandelot, where 600 cars assembled – an unheard-of number in those days. When Kayser and M. Magnien, the then Mayor of Meloisey,

FAR LEFT AND LEFT: *The Château of La Rochepot, the 15th-century castle which is one of the glories of the Hautes Côtes. Note the typical Flemish-influenced roofs.*

tried to promote tourism as a natural offshoot of their efforts, they found that their region was lacking every basic amenity, including roads between many of the villages – a deficiency which extended down to the Côte d'Or itself, for at the time even the road between Puligny and Meursault was just a dirt track. So, roads were built, and an embryonic *circuit touristique* established.

But it took twenty years or more to establish the wines. First came the founding of a cooperative, the only way to provide proper winemaking facilities. After a first attempt in 1955, when only 14 growers could be found to rally round the idea, during the 1960s the cooperative, sensibly sited on the outskirts of Beaune, really got off the ground. In 1967 Kayser retired as a schoolmaster to devote himself full-time to the cooperative, and by 1970 there were 70 members owning 100 hectares of vines, and a proper winery costing a million francs. By then the momentum was sufficient for the *syndicat* to encourage yet another crucial step which

108 remains almost unique in Burgundy, a *remembrement*, the regrouping of a ridiculously fragmented vineyard – a step that would have been impossible on the Côte d'Or, where the price of land was a hundred times that on the Hautes Côtes. After a 10-year struggle, Kayser also managed to convince the authorities to change the name of the *appellation* to the simpler Hautes Côtes de Beaune, with no mention of the fatal word "Bourgogne", which had previously reduced the wines' value.

Unfortunately, and not surprisingly given the region's unhappy history, the first generation of winemakers were looking for quantity above all and were not too bothered with ripeness – or quality of any sort for that matter. But now there's an irresistible combination of outside investment – often by venturesome firms like Faiveley and Antonin Rodet – and a new generation of winemakers. They are typified by the president of the joint *appellation*, Claire Naudin – young, qualified, a second-generation owner, whose father was a pioneer in re-establishing the vineyard. Today the Hautes Côtes have other things in their favour, apart from the warmer weather: the estates are relatively large and homogenous, and there are a number of second-generation enthusiasts working there, like Guy Simon.

The revolution is not confined to the Hautes Côtes, but is even more apparent on the Côte Chalonnaise. South of the little town of Chagny the landscape becomes more varied, though the underlying soils have the same Jurassic origins, albeit more gravelly and more diverse than in the Côte d'Or. But history was unfair to the vineyards on the slopes between Chagny and Tournus, as they were left out of the Côte d'Or *département*. Moreover, the five main wine communes in the region – Bouzeron,

In the not-so-distant past, this sort of mini-cottage – complete with well – would have housed cattle below and people above.

Rully, Mercurey, Givry and Montagny – have to fight their battles separately, since the generic *appellation*, Côte Chalonnaise, is of little use.

The unfairness is particularly apparent in Bouzeron, only a few kilometres south of Chagny and home to the most remarkable examples of the Aligoté grape in Burgundy, and therefore in the whole world of wine – there's only 250 hectares of the variety in Burgundy, and although there's lots in eastern Europe it's almost all pretty terrible stuff. The Aligoté was well represented on the Côte d'Or before the irresistible rise of the Chardonnay after 1945, which left it seeming rather ordinary in comparison. Its reputation for being enamel-strippingly acid – indeed it was once recommended in lieu of toothpaste – is merely reinforced by its fame as the basis for Kir, where the sweet blackcurrant liqueur offsets the assumed tartness of the wine. To Oz Clarke it has a

Pure Burgundian magic – autumnal morning mists over Volnay.

112 "fresh buttermilk flavour" with a "very refreshing bite balancing the often-appley fruit". I'm not sure about the buttermilk, but the crisp, Granny Smith bite is certainly, refreshingly, there – not toothpaste but clean, crisp fruiti-ness, with some mellowness given a year or two in bottle.

Bouzeron now has its own *appellation* attached to the variety thanks to a small group of growers headed by Aubert de Villaine, who has lived there since 1973 and makes probably the best Aligoté in the world, and by his neighbour Monsieur Chanzy. Their application was supported by the mayor of the little village, who just happened to be a senator. The vines are grown on two opposite slopes – east- and west-facing – near the village. Together they cover up to 80 hectares – there are another 20 hectares of less-good vines on the plateau above. The chalky slopes resemble those further north, but the top layer of soil is thin, which reins in the Aligoté's otherwise too exuberant growth, as does the "goblet" pruning (so named because it shapes the vines like the bowl of an upturned wine glass). In a normal year the two slopes balance each other out in stylistic terms, with the grapes on the east side providing the richer wines (although in 2001 they were almost wiped out by a hailstorm in August, resulting in an unbalanced vintage).

Rully, the next village south, also has its own speciality. For over a century and a half it has been best known for its sparkling wines. In 1822 a group of local landowners invited a young Champenois, François-Basile Hubert, to teach them to make their wines fizz – for were they not made of the same grapes as champagne itself? The tradition took on but the sparkling wines suffered badly in the great slump of the 1930s. Why buy Crémant de Bourgogne when real champagne was virtually being given away? But after the War one André Delorme, who had married a lady from Champagne, became intrigued by sparkling wine, and he and his son Jean-François, who still runs the firm, embarked on a long double job: of building up their own firm while trying to get the appropriate *appellation* for their sparkling wines. In 1975, after six years of efforts, they finally emerged with the name Crémant de Bourgogne. This is slightly misleading, for in Champagne the term *crémant* indicated a wine with only half the pressure of normal champagne, while Burgundy's version had the same force as champagne, not to mention a strength of character and a vinosity unusual in sparkling wines made outside the Champagne region.

So far as table wines are concerned, the figures tell the story of a tough struggle: of a long period of decay followed by a painful post-War recovery. In 1850 Rully had 600 hectares of vines, a figure which shrank to 250 by 1900. The lowest point was reached in 1945, when less than half of the 88 hectares of vines in the commune was entitled to the *appellation*. Even at the end of the 1960s, there were a mere 100 hectares – as against more than 200 today. And the presence of lots of young vines means that the reds in particular should continue to improve: at the moment most of them lack real individuality. Nevertheless, the slopes facing due east do produce wines of some bite and depth. The recovery owes quite a lot to Rully's deserved reputation as a source of good-value white wines – a reputation particularly encouraged

by Antonin Rodet, which leases the Château de Rully.

Mercurey is an irritating *appellation*. The reds in particular can be deep in colour and flavour and have what Jean-François Bazin describes as a sort of "rustic aristocracy". And the (less common) whites have enough acidity to be long-lasting. The best wines come from a golden bowl of south- and east-facing slopes which are the glory of the commune, sun-traps that provide the wines with their finesse. Unfortunately, for the usual political reasons, the name of Mercurey can be attached to wines from more than 600 hectares of vines, many growing on inevitably cold, wet and windy slopes facing west and even north.

To hear the story of some of the *appellation*'s best wines you have only to ask Michel Juillot and his son

LEFT AND RIGHT: *Burgundians have traditionally had green fingers and almost every house boasts its climbing plant (not necessarily a vine) and flowers, sometimes rising from a stone sink.*

Laurent, who has inherited his father's eloquence, force-fulness – and winemaking skills. Three generations have been able to expand the family's holdings – from a mere three hectares in 1946 to the 50 hectares they own today – simply because so few other buyers appreciated the vineyard's potential. But the going was tough. "It was my father who suffered the most," says Michel Juillot. He was not alone. Fortunately, many of the best sites are owned by Faiveley and Antonin Rodet, and today both firms are playing their proper role in promoting the commune's wines.

The smallest of the five communal *appellations* is Givry with 280 hectares of vines, but this is nearly three times the level of the late 1970s. Since then a serious effort of will on the part of the winemakers, helped by the inclusion of some well-respected vines in the commune of Jambles to the west of Givry, has made it a source of increasingly reliable, good-value, but not individualized, wines. Most of them are sold directly to

French customers, since the merchant community has never shown much interest in the commune.

The reputation of Montagny, the southernmost of the five, rather separate from the others, is limited by the fact that it is dominated by its cooperative which, like so many others, has no great ambitions for the wines it produces. Its name also suffers from a quirk of classification by which any of its (exclusively white) wines can be called Premier Cru if it reaches a certain alcohol level (11.5 per cent to be precise). Although far too high a proportion of the vineyard is classed above its quality, at their best its rich and minerally wines are reminiscent of the finest that Mâcon, just to the south, can produce.

A well-tended cottage lies between rows of similarly well-tended vines, with the route des vins *in the distance.*

amphitheatres of vines even more spectacular than those of Mercurey or Bouzeron. Despite these distinctive features, it has much the same ecclesiastical background as the rest of Burgundy – for example, its wines were once favoured by the monks of Cluny.

Most of the region – today occupying only 6,000 hectares, a third of the pre-phylloxera figure when its Gamays were known as the Grands Ordinaires de France – is devoted to the mass production of mediocre wines vinified by large cooperatives. On the southern edge near Mâcon itself is a complex mass of *appellations*, their vineyards dominated by two rock formations – Solutré and Vergisson. Solutré is the more dramatic and the better known, famous as a haunt of Cro-Magnon man, who left his tools behind, and more recently as the rock climbed by the late President Mitterrand every Easter with a chosen group of disciples. But it is the slopes of Vergisson which produce the better wines, because the vines face south and east. Elsewhere some of the vines face north or

To me, the Mâconnais – the name given to the region surrounding the town of Mâcon – is one of the most under-performing vineyards in France. It's an agreeably varied landscape, more reminiscent of rural France than of the monocultural heart of Burgundy to the north: its slopes sharper, its villages more picturesque, its

118 west, so the grapes rarely if ever ripen (so, Why are they entitled to the *appellation*? Don't ask me).

The most glamorous *appellation* is Pouilly-Fuissé, which had its fifteen minutes of fame in the 1970s when half its production went to the United States. But the Americans grew tired of over-sulphured, unbalanced wines from an *appellation* that refused to select any Premiers Crus from its finest sites on the assumption that they were all equally superior. Yet there are exceptions – for example, Jean-Jacques Vincent at the Château de Fuissé and his cousin Frédéric Burrier at the Château de Beauregard, whose best wines are fermented and aged in well chosen wood to give them real character.

By contrast, a relative newcomer, St-Véran, on the border between the chalky Mâconnais and the granite soils of Beaujolais, which received its own AOC only in 1971, has made its name through reliability and quality, even though many of its vines are young, so their wines will continue to improve for a decade or more. Today the wines from the south-facing slopes Les Terres Noires are rightly gaining an increasingly good reputation. St-Véran overshadows the two *appellations* it surrounds: the tiny and little-known Pouilly-Vinzelles and Pouilly-Loché – each of them toiling under the yoke of a cooperative. Yet in Viré-Clessé to the north, the cooperative has been a positive influence, its managers tenacious enough to have acquired an *appellation* for the vineyard, and open-minded enough to have taken its members to Britain, the most internationally competitive wine market in the world, to see what their rivals are like.

Even so none, but none, of the Mâconnais *appellations* can boast that its wines are, overall, as good as they ought to be, though everywhere there are enthusiasts showing what can be done, producing crisp, fruity reds from the Gamay and, above all, white wines of depth and character from the ubiquitous Chardonnay.

Training the vines high avoids damage from wet soil.

CHAPTER SIX

THE "OTHER" BURGUNDIES

THERE ARE TWO GREAT VINEYARDS AT THE EXTREME ENDS OF THE BURGUNDIAN SLOPES. A HUNDRED KILO-
METRES TO THE NORTH-WEST OF THE CÔTE D'OR LIES CHABLIS, A COMPACT REGION OF GENTLE SLOPES
AROUND THE RIVER SEREIN, PRODUCING DELICIOUS, CRISP — ALMOST STEELY — WHITE WINES, INEVITABLY
FROM THE CHARDONNAY. UNFORTUNATELY, IN RECENT YEARS THE VINEYARD HAS BEEN EXTENDED TOO FAR,
AND INFERIOR WINES HAVE DAMAGED ITS IMAGE. AND TO THE SOUTH, BETWEEN MÂCON AND THE GREAT
CITY OF LYONS, LIES BEAUJOLAIS, A VINEYARD SPECIALIZING IN FRESH, FRUITY WINES MADE FROM THE
GAMAY GRAPE, WHICH IS PLANTED VIRTUALLY NOWHERE ELSE IN THE WORLD. SINCE THE 1960s
BEAUJOLAIS HAS BECOME FAMOUS AS PRODUCER OF BEAUJOLAIS NOUVEAU, A FRESH WINE READY TO DRINK
A MERE COUPLE OF MONTHS AFTER THE HARVEST. BUT THE REGION — ABOVE ALL THE TEN *CRUS*, THE INDI-
VIDUAL VILLAGES ENTITLED TO PUT THEIR OWN NAME ON THE BOTTLE — CAN PROVIDE WINES THAT RETAIN
THEIR FRESHNESS, AND THEIR CHARACTERISTIC FRUITINESS, FOR YEARS.

122 Burgundy embraces two other wine-growing regions, which form a sort of framework, their contrasting wines providing examples of the enormous variety of the region's offerings. A hundred kilometres to the north-west of Dijon is Chablis with its fine, flinty white wines made from the ubiquitous Chardonnay. And just to the south of Mâcon, intermingling with the Mâconnais vine-yard, lies Beaujolais, producing very different wines from a granite soil not found elsewhere in Burgundy.

Beaujolais is the world's only major producer of wines made from that fruitiest of grapes, the *Gamay rouge au jus blanc* ("the red Gamay with white juice"), a variety probably brought to Burgundy from Dalmatia by the Roman emperor Probus. It's much juicier and higher-yielding than the Pinot, and, crucially, has much lower levels of tannin than any other major black grape variety. This makes its wines more immediately appealing than virtually any other red, but with less capacity to age. So it is generally underestimated because of the wine

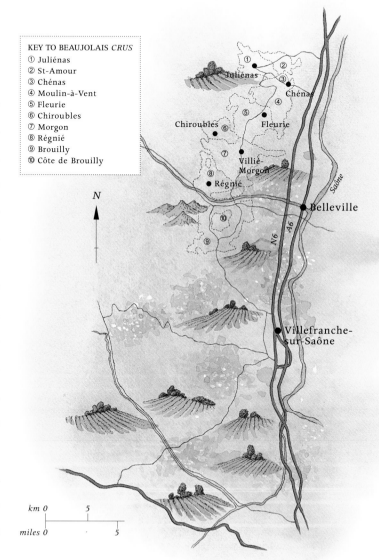

KEY TO BEAUJOLAIS *CRUS*
① Juliénas
② St-Amour
③ Chénas
④ Moulin-à-Vent
⑤ Fleurie
⑥ Chiroubles
⑦ Morgon
⑧ Régnié
⑨ Brouilly
⑩ Côte de Brouilly

N

km 0   5

miles 0   5

world's obsession with wines that can age for more than the five-year limit normal with Gamay – although it should benefit from the more recent obsession with "fruit-driven" wines, for no variety carries more of its fruitiness into the wine. A minority of the best Beaujolais can age well – all that happens is that the fruit gets more intense, more concentrated. Nevertheless, even the finest do not develop the deep, subtle secondary aromas found in mature bottles from "nobler" varieties.

(Beaujolais Blanc is very much a minority drink, which is a pity, because the small quantities of crisp, appley Chardonnay produced both in the extreme north, next to the Mâconnais, and in some chalky pockets in the south of the *appellation*, are worthy of wider renown.)

Geologically, Beaujolais divides pretty clearly into two halves. To the south of Villefranche, the soil is a mix of chalk and clay. To the north the slopes get steeper as you approach the Mâconnais and the villages become more picturesque, perched as they are on steep hillsides

124 well above the valley of the Saône. It is only to the north that you find the superior *appellation* Beaujolais Villages, which for fifty years has tried, successfully on the whole, to distinguish itself from the "ordinary" Beaujolais made in the south. Nevertheless, the Beaujolais Villages growers, like those to the south, still have a tendency to over-produce, averaging nearly 62 hectolitres (6,200 litres) of wine for every hectare, which is near the legal limit and above the level from which truly concentrated wines can be made. More scrupulous are the growers from the ten villages, all to the north, all in the steepest valleys, each entitled to its own *appellation*. These wines show the depth derived from their granitic hillside vineyards, and some of them can even absorb a bit of wood from the cask.

Unfortunately, the Gamay – and thus Beaujolais – has never really recovered its standing in the six centuries

since Duke Philip the Bold banished it from Burgundy proper. Its modern reputation started modestly enough, as the table wine in the bistros of Lyons. Indeed, until after the War the region's turnips were more profitable than its wines. But in the 1960s and 1970s, it was not the ten *crus* that achieved fame, but rather Beaujolais Nouveau – virtually the only wine drinkable immediately after fermentation (it remains an ideal form of fruit juice for quaffing in the bleak days of late November and December). In the 1960s its fame was spread by Parisian journalists who had made the acquaintance of the wine when they took refuge in Lyons during the German

September, from a 15th-century wall painting in the church at Bagnot in Burgundy. The mural features every month of the winemaker's year, this one complete with a happy little paddler.

occupation. Sales were further boosted by the prize awarded for the best bistro serving Beaujolais by the Académie Rabelais, a small group of Parisian restaurateurs and journalists who met in Brouilly. At the same time the wine's famous catchphrase, "le Beaujolais Nouveau est arrivé" ("Beaujolais Nouveau has arrived"), was coined by the late Louis Orizet, a senior civil servant who loved and understood the region better than anyone.

In the mid-1970s Beaujolais Nouveau became the rage in London after an enterprising journalist, the late Alan Hall, organized the (totally artificial) race to get the first wine to London. Today, even though the vogue has died down in Britain (through over-familiarity and a plethora of wines that were rather too sharp), the habit of celebrating the new vintage, complete with the drummed-up excitement surrounding its arrival, has spread throughout the world. As a result sales of Beaujolais Nouveau have exploded, from 100,000 hectolitres in 1970 to 576,000 in 1986 – more than half the total production of ordinary Beaujolais. This was helpful for its producers, but gave a somewhat unfair impression of the region's potential – a charge than can be levelled at much basic Beaujolais in a region where acreage and yield have risen so fast.

It does not help that Beaujolais is terribly tricky to produce – especially Beaujolais Nouveau, apparently the simplest of wines. Despite twenty years of experiments, it has proved impossible to harvest by machine because even the most sophisticated will bruise or break the skins of the grapes. All Beaujolais is fermented in three layers. At the bottom of the vat is the juice from the bunches of grapes which have been emptied into the top, stems and all (hence the vegetal, leafy overtones only too prominent in inexpertly made young Beaujolais). Because there is liquid only in the bottom third of the vat, outside yeasts have to be introduced to trigger the fermentation. In the middle of the vat are bunches of grapes that are beginning to split, and at the top bunches of whole grapes, in which every grape enjoys its own micro-vinification

in an atmosphere containing an increasing proportion of carbon dioxide rising from below. Macerating in the presence of carbon dioxide rather than oxygen helps the juice retain its fruitiness, which is vital for a wine that has to be drinkable almost immediately.

Quaffable though Beaujolais Nouveau may be, it is the ten *crus* that are capable of producing wines of distinct – and distinctive – qualities. Top of the tree is Moulin-à-Vent, described as halfway between Beaujolais and Burgundy. At its best it is deeper and more long-lasting than any other Beaujolais. In its shadow lies the much smaller Chénas, which in the hands of growers like Pierre Perrachon of Château Bonnet has aromatic overtones of stewed cherries. All the other *crus* have their particularities: Fleurie is for easy drinking; Juliénas, supposedly, has aromas of peony – or, to me anyway, raspberries; Morgon

FAR LEFT: *Grapes are carefully dusted with fungicide to produce the perfect bunches* (LEFT).

128 has overtones of kirsch; while Chiroubles is one of the most aromatic of Beaujolais with aromas of raspberries and violets. Wines from Brouilly, its vineyards encircling the hill of the same name, have their own red-fruit qualities. The best, south- and east-facing, slopes of the hill produce the underrated Côte de Brouilly, with its distinctive minerally overtones – owing to the poverty of the soil and subsoil. In the hands of good winemakers, like Nicole Chanrion of Les Crozes or Claude Geoffray at the handsome Château Thivin, this can be a seriously deep-flavoured wine. More fashionable is St-Amour, peachy, with overtones of crisp redcurrants (its sales helped by an association with St Valentine!). Last comes the still-disputed latest addition, Régnié. Until 1988, when it became entitled to its own name, it was known mainly as the commune where the trade went to find the best Beaujolais Villages. Even today the merchants are a little hesitant, and indeed it's clearly not a long-lasting wine, albeit freshly, crisply fruity when young.

If Beaujolais Nouveau has been a mixed blessing, the same cannot be said of Georges Duboeuf, a man who dominates the region as does no other equivalent figure in France. His greatest asset is his remarkable palate, allied to a gently persuasive disposition and a seeming modesty which leads him to assert that his business has merely "grown with Beaujolais itself". He was the son of a small grower across the border in the Mâconnais. Starting as a broker, his first success came from selling his own wine and that of his neighbours to Paul Blanc, owner of the famous Chapon Fin restaurant in nearby Thoissey. By the late 1950s his reputation as a reliable supplier of the best wines of Beaujolais had been spread by the region's major restaurateurs and encouraged by a handful of Parisian journalists like Raymond Baudoin.

Duboeuf soon developed the policy that has enabled

Before mechanization, man-power on a treadmill had to be used to crush the grapes, as shown on this postcard from Beaujolais.

Les Vendanges
PRESSURAGE - Le Fouloir
C'est au moyen d'un volant muni de chevilles, placé sur l'un
des axes latéraux mobiles que l'on fait pression.

him to become the biggest and most reliable supplier of fine Beaujolais, with a proper respect for individual *terroirs*. Unlike most other merchants (not only in Beaujolais but in France generally), he developed democratic partnerships with innumerable growers, based on *vigneronnage*, the local version of crop-sharing. For Duboeuf has always been more than a mere buyer: he and his team, including his son Franck, were, and remain, guides, counsellors and friends to an increasing number of growers.

Despite the present problems, stemming from the way that Beaujolais – above all the basic *appellation* – has become too closely associated with Beaujolais Nouveau, the locals are making far more concerted efforts to improve their lot – and the quality of their wines – than in any other region in Burgundy. They are helped by a thirty-year-old competition, the Salon des Deux

RIGHT: *The best bunches can be small.* FAR RIGHT: *Harvesting, like most tasks in the vineyard, is back-breaking work.*

Bouteilles, held in Villefranche in early December each year. In 2001, in what resembled a village fête on a grand scale, complete with lots of kids tucking into endless crêpes, 900 tasters sampled more than 3,000 submissions to find the best wines from the most recent and from earlier vintages. The occasion not only helps to promote the best wines, it also allows the growers to see what can be done with their precious Gamay.

But now the UIVB (Union Interprofessionnelle des Vins de Beaujolais) is tackling the thorniest problem in French viticulture: ensuring that only properly made wines, typical of the region, can be sold with an official stamp. Until now, growers who taste their neighbours' wines have been reluctant to reject them, knowing that this spells financial disaster to the loser. So the UIVB has devised a system under which wines refused the "label" after three tastings are distilled into industrial alcohol, but the grower is paid the proper market price for acceptable wine. He or she is then given advice on how to

improve the following year's wines. If they do not show sufficient improvement, then the wine goes for distillation again, and this time the grower is paid much less.

And what is Duboeuf doing to add to his reputation and that of his cherished region? Well, at the age of 68 he is stepping back from the management of his firm in order to concentrate on producing super-Beaujolais – primarily from his beloved Moulin-à-Vent.

Fundamentally, Chablis should be a simple phenomenon: it is white wine made from Chardonnay grown on a small area of chalk-and-clay soil on the slopes above the aptly-named River Serein ("serene"). The best Chablis should have a hint of green, like a fine olive oil, and it must be crisp, deeply flavoured, flinty, minerally,

A postcard depicting old-time harvesting in Chablis with, in the background, the gentle slopes characteristic of the appellation.

its steely backbone covered, but not hidden, by concentrated fruit. It's almost as though nature had created the wine expressly to form an ideal partnership with oysters, or indeed with any other shellfish you have handy. The only real argument is whether oak should play any role in its production. There are many people who agree with Anthony Hanson that use of wood – especially new oak – will inevitably deform the wine's natural qualities and turn it into merely "another" white Burgundy, albeit an excellent one. By contrast, I believe that the judicious use of new oak is vital to allow the grapes to reach their full aromatic potential and thus to create a wine capable of lasting, as a good Chablis should, for up to ten years.

Historically, Chablis has suffered enormously from two problems: frosts and frauds. Chablis is such a northerly vineyard that spring frosts are a regular danger and can result in the complete destruction of the crop. The locals take elaborate precautions, using water sprays, braziers – or even helicopters (to keep the air moving). As

134 for fraud, well, as Hanson puts it, "Chablis is to wine what Corot is to paintings: three out of four are false." Although tighter regulations now prevent any sharp white wine from being labelled as "Chablis" (in Europe anyway), the vineyard's reputation now suffers from home-grown injuries: an over-extended vineyard and over-cropping, leading to severe dilution of the average quality of the wine.

The history of Chablis echoes that of Burgundy as a whole. It was founded as a Gallo-Roman "villa" before falling into the hands of successions of monks, most notably from the abbey of Pontigny, second daughter of the great house of Cîteaux which owned much of "historic" Chablis, the slopes now covered by the Grands and Premiers Crus. The monks also enjoyed a near-monopoly of the presses so vital to wine production. After the

Revolution the vines were handed out to most of the inhabitants of the commune. This democratic gesture left a legacy that has prevented the region from being dominated by just a handful of major owners. Fortunately Chablis's cooperative, La Chablisienne, founded as early as 1923, has invariably set an example of how to produce well-made wines typical of the region, an example important because it now vinifies up to a third of the wines of the *appellation*.

The soil on which "historic" Chablis had been based was "Kimmeridgian" limestone, named after the cliffs surrounding Kimmeridge Bay in Dorset on the south coast

ABOVE: *Vine cuttings, which are often very aromatic, can also make superb fuel for barbecues.* RIGHT: *And when they're burnt in the vineyard, the ashes provide excellent, organic fertilizer.*

of England. Indeed the 111 hectares of Grands Crus, "les sept sages" ("the seven wise men"), have always been concentrated within the commune of Chablis on the right bank of the Serein. As a result they benefit from excellent chalky *terroir* and the full south-eastern aspect so vital to ripening grapes in such a northerly vineyard. Their quality, however, suffers from the typical Burgundian problem of excessive fragmentation, which divides the Grands Crus into four hundred plots.

Ever since 1923 some Chablisiens had wanted to create a new zone, making Chablis from vines grown away from the basic Kimmeridgian limestone, and allowing other grape varieties, including the Aligoté. The argument intensified in the 1960s as demand grew for the wine – and thus for an extension of the *appellation*. The arguments were personified by the heads of the two opposing camps, both locally born, but neither remotely conforming to the traditional image of the grower. Leader of the anti-extensionists was William Fèvre, a brilliant civil servant who was creating one of the finest estates in the region; while the expansionists were represented by the ambitious Jean Durup, an accountant by profession, based in Paris. The growers' group he headed argued that, historically, a great deal of Chablis had been grown on *terroir* called "Portlandian" – named after another part of the Dorset coast.

In 1976 Durup's camp was declared the winner. Much of the land around his home village of Maligny was upgraded from Petit Chablis to Chablis and, after an unsuccessful appeal by the Fèvre camp, 1,562 hectares was also added to the vineyard of Petit Chablis, of which only 200 hectares ended up being planted with vines. Although the authorities have tried to limit the damage to the potential quality of the wine by restricting plantation rights, the harm had been done. Between 1970 and 1990 the vineyard more than quadrupled in size, from a mere 756 hectares to 3,500, making Chablis one of the few *appellations* in France that is considerably bigger than it

was before phylloxera, while production rose fivefold to more than 26 million bottles. For yields were increasing as a result of modern viticultural methods.

Many of the Premiers Crus also benefited (in terms of size anyway) and so are now larger, more scattered, more varied than they were, or ought to be. Nevertheless, there is a small group, headed by Fourchaume, Montée de Tonnerre, Mont de Milieu and Vaulorent, over which there is no argument – indeed there are some wines from Fourchaume that have the delicacy and concentration of the finest Grands Crus. Recently, however, many of the best growers have got together to set up a Charter of Quality and, with luck, this could help to restore the reputation of this sometimes superb wine.

A classic autumnal landscape – note the narrowness of the lane, for land is too precious to waste on roads.

PRACTICAL REFERENCE

There are hundreds of merchants and cooperatives in Burgundy and thousands of estates, so any attempt to choose a sample will inevitably rely on my personal experience. In the following lists I've tried to cover the whole region and to include a number of the smaller merchants as well as better-known names. In choosing estates I've concentrated on those offering wines from a number of different *appellations* (a full list of *appellations* and Grands Crus follows these supplier lists). Although the prices charged, and the small quantities produced, by some of the leading estates will undoubtedly limit access to their wines to a lucky few, it would be ridiculous to leave them out since they represent the very best that Burgundy can offer.

SELECTED MERCHANTS

JEAN-CLAUDE BOISSET This native of the region has built up a stable of major brands by buying often impoverished merchants. These include Bouchard Aîné et Fils (not to be confused with Bouchard Père et Fils), Jaffelin and Mommessin. Most of his wines are bland and inoffensive, albeit well made, though he is now making a major effort to offer wines of greater distinction.

BOUCHARD PÈRE ET FILS Long-established firm. Owner of the biggest, including some of the best, estates in the Côte d'Or. Since its takeover by Joseph Henriot (see pp.70–71), the firm has become a leader in the production of quality wines, reflecting the very varied *terroirs* from which they come. It also owns William Fèvre in Chablis.

CHAMPY The oldest firm in Burgundy, with price lists dating back to 1720 to prove it. For much of the 20th century, it was dominated by one M. Mérat, who, in Hanson's words, was "… an autograph collector, polo player and cavalry colonel … ensuring that an old-world leisured air survived in its Second Empire offices and cellars." In 1990 the firm was bought by the well-respected broker, Henri Meurgey, who also owns DIVA, an export broking firm which supplies reliable domaine-bottled wines from two hundred estates.

ANDRÉ DELORME Based in Rully and the best-known supplier of Crémant de Bourgogne. It is also known for excellent whites from the Côte Chalonnaise.

JOSEPH DROUHIN Since 1880, when Joseph Drouhin bought a long-established firm, the business has gone from strength to strength, especially since management was taken over by the then 23-year-old Robert Jousset-Drouhin in 1957. Not only does the firm have substantial holdings on the Côte d'Or itself, it also owns more than 30 hectares in Chablis, including some Premiers Crus. And it vinifies and distributes the finest dry white wine in the world, the Montrachet from the estate of the Marquis de Laguiche. The cession of control to its Japanese importers has not made any difference to the wines' quality.

GEORGES DUBOEUF Rightly, the most respected supplier of every type of Beaujolais (see also pp.128–33).

FAIVELEY A distinguished family firm based in Nuits-St-Georges with a spread of vineyards on the Côte d'Or. But the great achievement of François Faiveley, the current manager, is to make some of the finest wines from the firm's estates on some of the best sites in Mercurey.

VINCENT GIRARDIN Based in Santenay, Girardin, like Olivier Leflaive, is a relative newcomer. He insists on low yields, and control of vinification by buying grapes rather than wine.

LOUIS JADOT One of the handful of firms that are great as well as large, making 700,000 cases of wine annually, much of it reliable, basic stuff from the whole region – including Beaujolais, where Jadot owns the best estate in Moulin-à-Vent, as well as its major holdings on the Côte d'Or. Founded in 1859, the firm was superbly managed by André Gagey from the end of the Second World War until 1993, when it was taken on by his son Pierre-Henri and the winemaker Jacques Lardière. The change of ownership in 1985, when it

was bought by Kobrand, its American importers, has not affected the quality of the firm's wines at all – indeed it has financed a major investment programme, including a new winery in Beaune itself.

LABOURÉ-ROI Respected firm based in Nuits-St-Georges with a wide range of vineyards. A pioneer in forming partnerships with growers. Result: the wines taste of the communes they came from.

LOUIS LATOUR The only one of the "Big Five" that is still family-owned. Its white wines, especially those from Corton, are models of their kind. But Latour's reds are another matter. They are pasteurized to stabilize them, a process that inevitably restricts the development of their aromas – and is unnecessary if modern winemaking practices are followed. Unfortunately, however, the view that winemaking in Burgundy reached its peak in the 18th century seems to be still influential here.

OLIVIER LEFLAIVE Over the past 18 years, this scion of the Leflaive family (see

pp.92–5) has built up a deserved reputation as supplier of a wide range of reliable wines of a quality found in few longer-established merchants.

ÉTABLISSEMENTS LORON ET FILS Large-scale and eminently reliable supplier of a full range of Beaujolais.

OLIVIER MERLIN A newcomer based in the tiny village of La Roche-Vineuse making some of the most interesting wines in the Mâconnais – both from his own estate (Domaine du Vieux St-Sorlin) and, increasingly, from bought-in grapes.

PATRIARCHE PÈRE ET FILS Until recently the firm was best known for its Kriter sparkling wine, for its well-placed cellars in Beaune (particularly the Couvent des Cordeliers and the Marché aux Vins), and for the fine wine it makes at the Château de Meursault. But the new generation that has taken over since the death of long-standing owner André Boisseaux in 1993 is steadily improving Patriarche's other offerings.

ANTONIN RODET Based in Mercurey, the firm has naturally specialized in impeccable, good-value wines from the Côte Chalonnaise. Among the estates it owns or manages are the Château de Chamirey (source of one of the best whites in Mercurey), the Château de Rully, and the Château de Mercey in the Hautes Côtes. Under the management of Bertrand Devillard, the firm's winemakers are allowed to go their own way – one of the best, Nadine Gublin, has worked miracles with the previously under-performing Domaine Jacques Prieur in Meursault.

SELECTED COOPERATIVES

CAVE DES VIGNERONS DE BUXY One of the technical show-places of Burgundy, this large (its members own 750 hectares of vines) cooperative in the heart of the Côte Chalonnaise is offering increasingly satisfying wines.

LA CHABLISIENNE Enormous cooperative accounting for a third of the production of Chablis. One of the few in Burgundy to maintain a high standard even in its ordinary offerings.

CAVE DE VIRÉ-CLESSÉ The unusually open-minded and quality-conscious management is largely responsible for the creation of the new *appellation* Viré-Clessé, and produces clean, fruity, good-value wines typical of the region.

SELECTED ESTATES

DOMAINE DU MARQUIS D'ANGER-VILLE An outstanding estate in Volnay of considerable historic importance (see p.82). Its wines are outstanding thanks to the quality of the vineyards – including the single-owned Premier Cru, Clos des Ducs – and the care taken over winemaking.

JEAN-MARC BOILLOT As a grandson of Étienne Sauzet, he demanded his share of the family vineyards in Pommard and has shown himself worthy of his inheritance.

MICHEL BOUZEREAU The best of the half dozen or so Bouzereaus making wine in Meursault – and producer of an outstanding Aligoté from Bouzeron.

DOMAINE CHANDON DE BRIAILLES In 1989 the Chandon family (as in Moët & Chandon) took back the estate, which has vines in many of the best sites of the Côte de Nuits. It produces brilliant wines, largely thanks to Claude de Nicolay, one of the few Burgundian winemakers to have worked in the New World.

DOMAINE GÉRARD CHAVY ET FILS Classic wines from Puligny-Montrachet needing time to show at their best.

DOMAINE BRUNO CLAIR Historic family estate on the Côte de Nuits reborn after its takeover by the open-minded Bruno Clair in 1989.

J.-F. COCHE-DURY Produces some of Burgundy's most sought-after wines from vineyards both north and south of Beaune (in Corton and Meursault respectively), most of them going to the best restaurants in France.

DOMAINE DUJAC A legend in Burgundy for the wines and for the questing spirit of Jacques Seysses, maker of elegant, flavoursome wines from all along the Côtes de Nuits.

DOMAINE WILLIAM FÈVRE Built up since the 1950s by the eponymous M. Fèvre (see p.136) and now owned by Bouchard Père et Fils, its wines are invariably fine examples of the judicious use of wood in making fine, long-lasting Chablis.

DOMAINE JEAN GRIVOT Owner of some marvellous vineyards that are carefully tended by Étienne Grivot.

DOMAINE MICHEL GROS Low yields and a judicious proportion of new oak ensure great wines from an historic estate with vines in Vosne-Romanée and Nuits-St-Georges.

BERNARD HUDELOT The outstanding winemaker in the Hautes Côtes – his impressive wines command prices far above those obtained by his neighbours'.

DOMAINE JACKY JANODET One of Beaujolais's rare "superstars" based, like Georges Duboeuf, in Romanèche-Thorins, and making firm, seductive wood-aged wines from Moulin-à-Vent and St-Amour.

HENRI, GEORGES AND LUCIEN JAYER AND NEPHEW EMMANUEL ROUGET The arrangements within this family are complicated. The star is Henri, a fanatic for clean culture and low yields, whose wines are fought over by connoisseurs the world over.

DOMAINE MICHEL JUILLOT Excellent-value red and white wines from one of the outstanding growers in Mercurey.

DOMAINE DES COMTES LAFON According to Anthony Hanson this Meursault estate's white wines "... often surpass, in complexity, potential and deliciousness, Grands Crus from lesser wine-makers in Chassagne or Puligny."

DOMAINE LAROCHE Rapid expansion since 1975 has not diluted the quality of Michel Laroche's offerings of Chablis from most of the best *crus*.

DOMAINE LEROY The newest, and most extraordinary, major estate in Burgundy, created by the formidable Lalou Bize-Leroy after she left the family property of the Domaine de la Romanée-Conti in 1991. Buying a dozen parcels of the finest vines, and switching (not without some problems) to bio-dynamic cultivation, she now produces wines of awesome depth – and even more awesome prices.

DOMAINE MÉO-CAMUZET The estate was built up by Étienne Camuzet, local *député* between the wars and donor of the Château du Clos de Vougeot to the Chevaliers du Tastevin. The domaine produces rich, unfiltered, long-lasting wines from the Côte de Nuits and is now lovingly taken care of by Camuzet's great-nephew Jean Méo, a former industrialist.

DOMAINE MICHELOT Now run by Bernard Michelot and his son-in-law Jean-François Mestre. It offers a wide range of

wines, including good simple *bourgogne blanc*, though yields, even of the best wines, are said to be a little on the high side.

HUBERT DE MONTILLE A Dijon lawyer deeply involved in vinous litigation (and in wine), with a number of extremely well-sited plots in Volnay and Pommard. He and his son Étienne, who has taken over the estate, are both strong advocates of restraint in chaptalization (adding sugar to increase alcohol content), so that their wines stay true to their *terroir*.

NAUDIN-FERRAND Claire Naudin (see also p.108) offers a wide range of well-made wines from the Hautes Côtes.

DOMAINE FERNAND ET LAURENT PILLOT Old vines, and careful fermentation and maturation, from a 14-hectare estate in Chassagne ensure classic wines.

CHÂTEAU DE POMMARD Twenty whole hectares in single ownership, a record for Burgundy. Its owner Jean-Louis Laplanche is one of France's best-known

psychoanalysts. Using traditional viticultural methods, including tight pruning and low yields, he makes the most of his inheritance.

DOMAINE RAMONET As Hanson says, "a place of pilgrimage" for any lover of domaine-bottled Burgundy. In the 1930s Pierre Ramonet's wines became legendary in the USA as well as in France. Nowadays, the estate's reputation for total integrity is maintained by brothers Jean-Claude and Noël Ramonet.

DOMAINE DE LA ROMANÉE-CONTI Far and away the greatest estate in Burgundy (see pp.54–5).

DOMAINE SAUZET In the forty or so years before he died in 1975, Étienne Sauzet built up one of the most prominent estates in Burgundy. His grandson-in-law Gérard Boudot has maintained the estate's reputation with some interesting Premier Cru plots in Puligny and Chassagne and now also buys grapes and must (grape juice) from other growers.

GUY SIMON ET FILS Well-established grower in the Hautes Côtes making some of the best wines from the *appellation*.

DOMAINE DU COMTE GEORGES DE VOGÜÉ A major estate owning 70 per cent of the Grand Cru Musigny and nearly 20 per cent of Bonnes-Mares. Now making wine worthy of the *terroir*.

APPELLATIONS AND GRANDS CRUS

REGIONAL APPELLATIONS
Bourgogne
Bourgogne Aligoté
Bourgogne Chitry
Bourgogne Clairet *or* Bourgogne Rosé
Bourgogne Côte Chalonnaise
Bourgogne Côte du Couchois
Bourgogne Côte St-Jacques
Bourgogne Côtes d'Auxerre
Bourgogne Coulanges-la-Vineuse
Bourgogne Épineuil
Bourgogne (Grand) Ordinaire
Bourgogne Hautes-Côtes de Beaune
Bourgogne Hautes-Côtes de Nuits
Bourgogne Mousseux

Bourgogne Passe-Tout-Grains
Bourgogne Vézelay
Crémant de Bourgogne
Mâcon
Mâcon (plus name of village)
Mâcon Supérieur
Mâcon-Villages
Pinot-Chardonnay-Mâcon

COMMUNAL APPELLATIONS
Aloxe-Corton
Auxey-Duresses
Beaune
Blagny
Bouzeron
Chablis (and Chablis Premier Cru)
Chambolle-Musigny
Chassagne-Montrachet
Chorey-lès-Beaune or Chorey
Côte de Beaune
Côte de Beaune-Villages
Côte de Nuits-Villages
Fixin
Gevrey-Chambertin
Givry
Irancy
Ladoix
Maranges
Marsannay
Marsannay Rosé

Mercurey
Meursault
Montagny
Monthélie
Morey-St-Denis
Nuits-St-Georges or Nuits
Pernand-Vergelesses
Petit Chablis
Pommard
Pouilly-Fuissé
Pouilly-Loché
Pouilly-Vinzelles
Puligny-Montrachet
Rully
St-Aubin
St-Romain
St-Véran
Santenay
Sauvignon de St-Bris
Savigny-lès-Beaune or Savigny
Viré-Clessé
Volnay
Volnay-Santenots
Vosne-Romanée
Vougeot

GRANDS CRUS
Bâtard-Montrachet
Bienvenues-Bâtard-Montrachet
Bonnes-Mares

Chablis Grand Cru
Chambertin
Chambertin-Clos de Bèze
Chapelle-Chambertin
Charlemagne
Charmes-Chambertin
Chevalier-Montrachet
Clos de la Roche
Clos de Tart
Clos de Vougeot
Clos des Lambrays
Clos St-Denis
Corton
Corton-Charlemagne
Criots-Bâtard-Montrachet
Échezeaux
Grands Échezeaux
Griotte-Chambertin
La Grande Rue
La Romanée
La Tâche
Latricières-Chambertin
Mazis-Chambertin
Mazoyères-Chambertin
Montrachet
Musigny
Richebourg
Romanée-Conti
Romanée-St-Vivant
Ruchottes-Chambertin

ACKNOWLEDGMENTS

AUTHOR'S ACKNOWLEDGMENTS

In writing this book I am aware of reposing on the sturdy shoulders of two giants, both friends: in London Anthony Hanson, author of the authoritative work on the subject; and in Burgundy Jean-François Bazin, author, journalist, politician, and the most loving, knowledgeable and irresistibly quotable of guides. I am also grateful for the support of Jean-Charles Servant and Nellie Blau of the Bureau Interprofessionnel des Vins de Bourgogne (BIVB) and Anne Masson of the Union Interprofessionnelle des Vins du Beaujolais (UIVB).

At my publishers I was lucky to find Bob Saxton, James Hodgson (a meticulous but not nagging editor), and Emma Rose (a superb book designer).

LIST OF WORKS CITED

pp.14–16, 29, 91 Cyrus Redding, *A History and Description of Modern Wines*, London, 1833

pp.29–31, 88, 91, 93 Simon Loftus, *Puligny-Montrachet*, Ebury Press, London, 1992

p.43 André Védel et al, *Essai sur la dégustation des vins*, INAO, Mâcon, 1972

p.48 Jean-François Bazin, *Le Vin de Bourgogne*, Hachette, Paris, 1996

pp.63, 68, 80, 134, 138, 141, 142 Anthony Hanson, *Burgundy*, Faber and Faber, London, 1995 (second edition)

pp.88, 112 Oz Clarke and Margaret Rand, *Grapes and Wines*, Websters International Publishers, London, 2001

p.88–91 Claude Arnoux, *Dissertation sur la situation en Bourgogne*, London, 1728

PICTURE CREDITS

The publishers would like to thank the following people and photographic libraries for permission to reproduce their material. Every care has been taken to trace copyright holders. However, if we have omitted anyone we apologize and will, if informed, make corrections in any future edition.

p.13 Musée du Vin de Bourgogne, Beaune/Art Archive, London/Dagli Orti

p.27 Abbey of St Philibert, Tournus/Bridgeman Art Library, London

p.36 Bibliothèque Municipale, Dijon/AKG, London/ Erich Lessing

p.54 Collection Confrérie des Chevaliers du Tastevin, Nuits-St-Georges

p.61 Hôtel-Dieu, Beaune/Bridgeman Art Library, London

p.66 Frans Hals Museum, Haarlem/Bridgeman Art Library, London

p.73 Musée du Vin de Bourgogne, Beaune/Art Archive, London/Dagli Orti

p.124 Church, Bagnot/AKG, London/Jean-Paul Dumontier

p.129 Collection Georges Duboeuf, Romanèche-Thorins

p.132 Private Collection